THE LOCK IS BROKEN

2007-2014
GOD'S END TIME PROPHECIES REVEALED

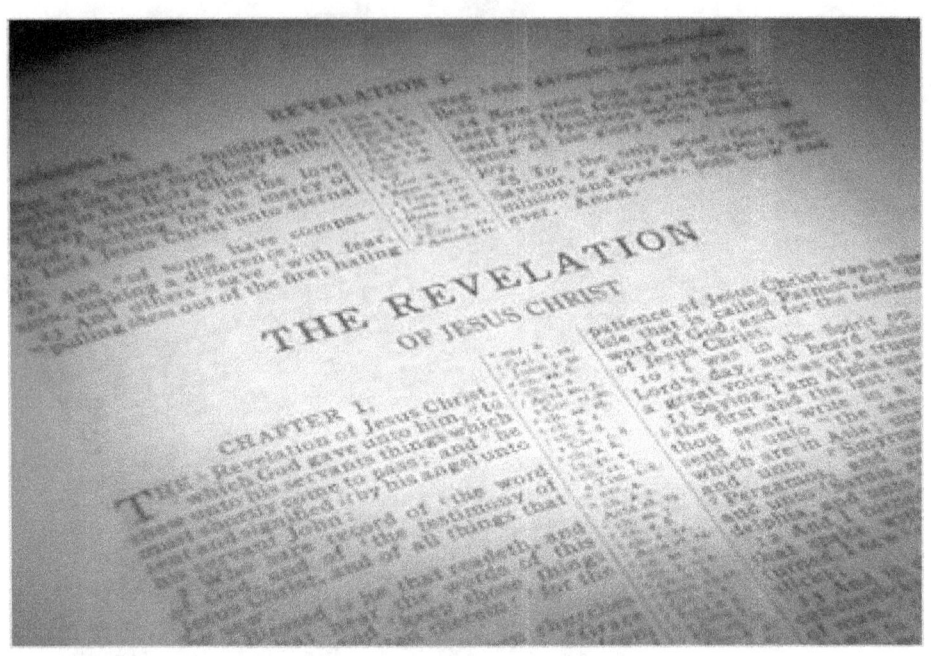

END TIME PROPHECIES UNFOLD

2007 – 2014

By

Prophet Christ Mondzali

Prophet's Testimony of GOD

John 5:30-36

V-30: I can of mine own self do nothing, as I hear I judge and my judgment is just; because I seek not mine own will but the WILL of the father which hath sent me

V-31: If I bear witness of myself, my witness is not true

V32: There is another that beareth witness of me and I know that the witness which he witnesseth of me is true

V33: Ye sent unto John, and he bare witness into the truth

V34: But I receive not testimony from man: but these things I say, that ye might be saved

V35: He was a burning and a shining light: and ye were willing for a season to rejoice in his light

V36: But I have greater witness than that of John: for the works which the father hath given me to finish, the same works that I do bear witness of me, that the Father hath sent me.

- "All scripture is given by inspiration (or revelation) of GOD, and is profitable for doctrine, for reproof, for correction, for instruction in righteousness..." **2Timothy 3:16**
- *"And He saith unto me: "Seal not the sayings of the prophecy of this book: for the Time is at hand." Revelation 22:10*
- "I will stand upon my watch, and set me upon the tower, and will watch to see what he will say unto me, and what I shall answer when I am reproved.
- And the Lord answered me, and said: Write the vision; make it plain upon tables, that he may run that readeth it. **For the vision is yet for an appointed time**, but at the end it shall speak, and

not lie: though it tarry, wait for it: because it will surely come, it will not tarry." **Habakkuk 2:1-4**

- ***"And it shall come to pass afterward***, that I will pour out my spirit upon all flesh: and your sons and yours daughters shall prophesy, your old men shall dream dreams, your young men shall see visions: And also upon the servants and upon the handmaids in those days will I pour out my spirit. " **Joel 2:28-29**
- **"Write the things which thou hast seen, and the things which are, and the things which shall be hereafter" Revelation 1:18**

Acknowledgements

I wish to express my deepest appreciation to **my wife, *Bernadette***, for her constant support, encouragement and prayers, and to my friends in Christ who really played a role in this journey of writing this book: Sister **Mhay. Biggs** and Husband **Bryan Biggs** for their contribution and support.

To the body of Christ, because of you the Lord has inspired his servant these revelations for you to come to the knowledge of events ahead and get prepare for his return.

I am deeply happy to know for a fact that JESUS is the only one in control of all the events unfold in this book and that when you go through this book and study deeper, you will never again be the same.

I am grateful to the Holy Spirit for helping me understand with clarity of spirit each revelation given and enabling me to properly and positively present to the body of Christ this glorious end time revelations, touching the church, the Rapture, the nations of the world, America, Israel and his enemies the kingdom of GOD and upcoming events of One World Government (New World Order & Co). All the Glory unto GOD the Father of our Lord and Savior Jesus Christ.

I am extremely and beyond measure blessed that He has chosen me for this end time assignment.

Approach this book with prayer each time you go through chapters, inviting the Holy Spirit to guide you in all wisdom, knowledge and understanding of His revelations...in doing so the enemy of your soul (Satan) would have no power or dominion upon you.

CONTENTS *of* Chapters

Prophet(Christ Mondzali) Testimony of God

Acknowledgements

1. Christ, The Rock of ages
   - The Cross, Focus of prophecy
2. Mystery of the 3 Crosses at Golgotha
3. The Rapture
   - Three prophetic events for the end time season
4. March of prophecy: The graph
5. The prophetic Calendar of GOD
   - Hebrew Calendar 2011-2012 as an example
   - The Feast of the Lord
6. The Prophetic Alphabet
7. 2008, Year of Jubilee Revealed
8. The 3 Major covenants in the Bible
   - Glimpse on what is A Vow?
9. The Law of Becoming
10. The Coming Financial Earthquake 2008-2014
11. 5 Majors Crises (2008-2014)
12. The Name BARAK in Prophecy
    - Daniel 7 Revealed
13. America in prophecy
14. The Spirit of Ancient Empires in America
15. The War of GOG and MAGOG in Prophecy
16. The Kingdom of the Antichrist Forming
17. GOD and the Ministry of Angels
    - Angels Ministering spirits

18. The Pre-Adamic World
    - The Curse after the Fall and the Five Underworlds
19. Classification of Demons by Month
20. Why GOD is So Serious with You?
    - Strike your enemy 100% to Death

2011-2014: Season of God's Eagles

CHRIST, the Rock of Ages

The Cross, Focus of prophecy.

Exodus 17:3-7 (read from Verse 1)

Moses conducting his people through the desert is now challenged to give them water. After crying unto the Lord, let's see what happened to them.

v-6: God said: I will stand before thee upon the rock in horeb, and thou shall smite the rock...Jesus is called the "Rock of Ages" because HE IS form the beginning of ages that ROCK.

Now here, Jesus is the one prophetically standing on that rock which Moses his servant is about to smite with a rod. Amen!

The bible says in Isaiah 53:5" by his Stripes we are healed" Because He was wounded and bruised upon the cross, He brought out Salvation(river of Living Water) therefore the people of Israel could experience Salvation through the water out of the Rock. Here we see already the way Almighty God prepared the Way.

Now, before we proceed further, let's examine also Exodus 15:22-26 where we find for the first time Israel thirsty .Here in this chapter, they could not drink of the waters of MARAH which means BITTER.

V 25: The Lord revealed to Moses the prophet a tree, which, when it has been cast into the waters, the waters were made sweet and drinkable.

Listen:

1) The waters of MARAH represent here the hearts of men, with bitterness. The Bible says who can heal the hearts, only GOD.

2) The tree here (which by revelation of the word is a Green Tree) represents the Cross. You may say how do you know that that green tree is the cross? Well, the Holy Spirit led me to read in parallel Luke 23:31 and I came to the revelation and knowledge that the Piece of Tree that was placed upon the Master to carry on to Golgotha was in fact a fresh green tree. As you know a green Tree is full of water and therefore heavy. This may also explain why the Lord was falling several times on his way to Calvary. Only the Cross of Jesus can circumcise the heart of men and bring it unto true repentance.

Praise the Lord! Now the Holy Spirit is showing me some powerful things.

This chapter, in a prophetic way shows exactly what the Lord Jesus Christ will go through when the time was ready; it unfold by itself the Plan of redemption of men by GOD Himself. Remember in the gospel he carried his cross John 19:17; Mark 15:17-24 through (in) the waters of Marah (People of the city), but by doing so Luke 23:27-31 the Hearts of men (waters of Marah) were redeemed or purified)…again read Isaiah 53:1-5.

<<The Rock of Ages talks about the Cross and how out of Jesus' body, water of eternal life came out and brought Salvation to men kind>>.

Three times, the servant of GOD Moses, will struggle with the water' problem (salvation of Israel) because water is LIFE (only Jesus could Give); also three times Jesus will deal with the cross. Let's go a little deeper and examine this together:

1) Exodus 15:23-26 -→ Luke 23:27-31
2) Exodus 17:6-7 -→ Isaiah 53:3-5 & Luke 23:33-43(also Luke 14:25-27)
3) Numbers 20:5-11 -→ John 19:33-37

By reading more scriptures, more revelations will come unto you, allow me to give some here: by comparison all truth is parallel.

Deuteronomy 32:4; Psalms 78:15-22

Psalms 95:1-8; Psalms 28:1;

Psalms 62:2; John 7:37-39;

1Corinthians 10:4-12

The Mystery of the 3 Crosses at Golgotha

Luke 23:39-43

What qualifies you today is not your bank account, nor your beauty or Knowledge.

What qualifies you is not your new Cadillac or Chrysler, I should even say not your mansion on the beach of Malibu or your position and name in this society …But you are qualified because over 2000 years ago, someone die on the cross and His name IS J.E.S.U.S of Nazareth.

For many years I could not understand why on that very particular day, when the Master die only 3 crosses were lifted up on Golgotha as if it was just by coincidence. So you may ask the question: why 3 crosses? I'm glad you ask! Now let's discover the revelation or plan of GOD from the Old Testament reading Exodus 12:1-6

First of all, let me give you this revelation:

From the day Jesus entered the Temple in Jerusalem and threw away the dealers and sellers of pigeons, until his crucifixion there is four (4) days. He entered on the 9th month, the 10th day and died on the 14th.

Look at this: 4 days: on the 4th day and 3 days later he rose from the death, that's gives a total of 7 days: God's Perfection.

Ok, back to Exodus 12.

Examining the sketch on Golgotha, we see two criminals who are sentenced to death penalty. On that particular day was the

Passover and they "needed to be saved", (to pass over meaning death should pass over they heads).One was the neighbor next to Jesus, he believed right there that JESUS was the lamb of GOD ready (roasted see exodus 12:8) to be eaten therefore be save(Here I'm paraphrasing with rhetoric and symbolic words to make you see the parallel between those two events in the O.T and N.T).By confessing the name of JESHUAH, he was justified and saved(accepted into GOD's kingdom), but the other one, rejecting JESUS(did not partake at the table of the Lamb) was condemned and judged and died without hope.

See the analogy that follows: Verse 4

The Lamb is JESUS

The 1st prisoner: Neighbor (you & me, symbolizing Christian partakers of the Lamb's table). Galatians 2:20 says: " I am (Neighbor or Prisoner) crucified with Christ : nevertheless I live; yet not I, but Christ liveth in me: and the life which I now live in the flesh I live by the faith of the Son of God, who loved me, and gave himself for me."

The 2nd Prisoner: Egyptian (The World, far away from the Lamb's table refusing his free gift of salvation).1 John 5:12 says "He who has the Son has life; he who does not have the Son of God does not have life."

We can now see clearly that father GOD planed this scenario of the 3 Crosses way before to fulfill his purpose and plan when the time comes, talking about JESUS Christ his only son.

The 10th day was Sunday, first day of the week.

4 days later makes it the 14th, the day of preparation and corresponds on Thursday.

The 15th was Friday, Jesus is already in the tomb (grave); but Friday was the Feast of unleaved bread: see Leviticus 23:6-7 which is the Sabbath and go till the 16th which is in this case the Regular Sabbath.

The 17th was the feast of the First Fruits which is The Resurrection. Now we understand why Jesus is called the first fruit of the creation and therefore He ought to rise that very day (John 20:1). Wow! This is great!

Now say with me out loud: *"I've got the DNA of the Almighty GOD in me, I have the blood of a champion." You are God's Masterpiece.*

No one can make you feel inferior without your permission. Your attitude will put you UP or DOWN, HIGH or LOW. Let me advise you to check your birth certificate, because the last time I checked mine it says: redeemed by the blood of the Lamb and highly favored.

The RAPTURE

The Profile and Foreshadow of events

Already in the old testament the Lord GOD revealed and talked about this great future event. It is in my opinion one of the greatest revelation I have ever had from HIM. As you continue to read, your mind will be blow away.

Exodus 19:10

The Lord instructed Moses his servant to sanctify the people for 2 days which represents the church age...by prophetic interpretation 2days= 2000years.

The message was that the people were to be sanctified and prepared for the 3rd day. These verses give us both a profile of the rapture of the church and a parallel to the second advent of Jesus Christ. Keep reading!

V-16: The morning of the 3rd day

The voice of the trumpet not a sound, wait a minute, trumpet does not have voice but give sound, so here it's about a being(angel) for you to grasp this compare with first book of Thessalonians 4:16-17

Now in Exodus 24:16-18 , touching the transfiguration, Moses the servant of GOD went up into the cloud after six days, just like Jesus who took Peter, James and John to a High Mountain in Matthew 17:1-3 and there, they experienced the " Rapture scenario" of Elijah, Jesus and Moses which are the composite of the rapture.

Now if you apply the principle that 1day equal 1000 years, this again confirm that the rapture is to be after 6000 years from the time of Adam.

Let's compare Mat 17:1-3 and Rev21:10 also 2 Peter1:16-18...it says in the gospel they went to a literal mountain but got into a spiritual vision and caught up into a holy mountain of God(New Jerusalem)...let me give you something to dig deeper:

Moses has been dead 1500 years under the Old Testament or covenant and when the righteous died they went down in paradise (which at that time was in the heart of the earth see Mat 12:40) in other words was called by the Jewish Abraham's bosom .Luke 16:26 and Ephesian 4:8-9

After the creation GOD gave Adam & Eve a lease on planet Earth for 6000 years: Genesis 1:26-28 Just as Isaiah the Prophet Prophesied in Isaiah 46:9-10;

Man has to exercise dominion but after that season is over GOD will take back control of the earth: Psalms 24:1

Let's go deeper with Genesis 29:15-28

Jacob has to marry Rachel the promised one, but instead Laban gave him first of all Lea , Rachel's sister; then he has to work or labor for Laban 7 years before finally having his loved one RACHEL.

The Bible says Jacob went through 7 years of trouble before the 7 years of harvest and peace. Therefore, we the church (Rachel) is expecting the Rapture and GOD kept these end time events in perfect numerical order.

Watch this:

Do you know that an Hebrew servant was to serve his master six(6) years and be set free or released on the 7th year? Exodus 21:2

Joshua marched around Jericho with 7 priest blowing 7 trumpets and they turned around 7 times before the fortress collapsed? Joshua 6:3-4.

Jacob is the type of Jesus and he has 12 sons which are type of twelve (12) disciples also symbolized the Authority. Ruben was his first born and Judas the first tribe of Israel.

Get ready because we are taking off now:

God revealed to me mighty things so let's focus on Moses again in Deuteronomy 34:1-7 and now let's read 2 Kings 2:1-11. You do that and I will break it down prophetically for you in a moment but first:

Back to Genesis 6:3 the 120 jubilee years correspond to 6000 years; well how do I get it?

Listen between Adam and Abraham there is 2000 years, between Abraham and Jesus, 2000 years and between Jesus and the Church today,2000 years; Each 2000 years = 2days also. According to GOD's mathematic 1day=1000 years but later in this book I will break it in detail with a graph, talking about the March of Prophecy.

Therefore 40 years=40 jubilee years which are 2000 years; now to have 120 jubilee years you have to multiply 40 by 3(prophetic number of Trinity) and get 120 years.

6000 years = 6days of Creation meaning also that the lease is for 6000 years, because on the 7th day (Sabbath) The Lord GOD rested. Brethren we are about to enter into His Rest as well.

Talking about Deuteronomy 34:1-7 the last book of Moses, He died when he reached 120 years…Many preachers and pastors and prophets never really went deeper into that period of time and question why Moses a mighty prophet of GOD will die only 120 years, He was too young compare to Noah or even Adam. Some said that because He sinned against God by killing the Egyptian or in the desert when smiting the Rock with anger…All of these theories may be right on one hand, but let me bring you the great revelation ever on the other hand: All these revelations given to me by the Holy Spirit started in the year 2008, a year and half after I came to this country.

He died to fulfill the prophecy of GOD, I should say God's Prophetic agenda of the end time season marked by the Rapture. In God's agenda, Moses represents the righteous Dead and Elijah the Righteous Alive or the Body of Christ or the church caught up after 6 days or 6000 years; but let's move one step at the time.

What is amazing and interesting is that by revelation the Spirit of the Lord came upon me and revealed to me that the archangel Michael is responsible of that great event: the Rapture. What? You may wonder!

Moses is died in the plain of Moab, just before the Jordan river and Canaan the promised land…But over 500 years later , The Lord God has his plan going on when He chose one prophet Elijah in 2 Kings 2:1-11 and send him exactly at the same location where the first one fall and be picked up by chariots of fire. Let's have a close look at that event: The Spirit of Revelation came upon me and this is what he revealed to me:

The reason why Elijah is sent to that area is first for Michael to pick up the body of Moses at the plain of Moab then Pick up Elijah at the Jordan river...See deeper now: The only time Michael is mention in the Bible coming down on earth is in this segment of the word in Jude 9 where we see Michael disputing with Lucifer over the body of Moses, confirming the revelation on that very day He came to pick up Moses. He is the one

Who came and took Elijah in a chariot of fire...because of the nature of the anointing of Elijah the prophet of Fire psalms 68:17,psalms 104:3-4; 2 chronicles 5:13-14; Colossians 1:27 and Romans 8:17-18.

Interesting to see that the Lord GOD sent him at the same place where Moses was buried and be caught up together: See Jude 9; 1 Thessalonians 4:16-17 and Matt 17:1-3.

Now open wide your spirit...

If Elijah represents the body of Christ (Church) caught up , therefore the spirit of Elijah has been given to the church and GOD kindle us with his spirit unto flame of fire.

That why Jesus came with the spirit of Elijah in Matt 3:11.hecame with the Holy Ghost and Fire; when He ascended in heaven he gave us the spirit of Elijah, to be witnesses of powerful miracles, only manifest by and through the baptism of fire...read Malachi 4:5-6

In verse 6 of Malachi the 4th chapter it says: ...And shall turn the heart of the fathers...

Matt 11:14-17; Luke 1:17 cannot explain nothing else than signs and wonders that follow them that believeth in Jesus Christ.

The word **_Dynamus_** which means **_Power_** has been received by the church with the spirit of fire from Elijah the prophet of Fire. When you compare both scriptures: Malachi 4:5-6 is the parallel of Luke 1:17, it's all about the Church.

Three Prophetic Events for the end time Season

MARK 5:1-43

V-9: The term Legion here means 6000 foot soldiers in the roman's army.

The Lord Jesus faces three major events as He enter the city, unfolding the upcoming end time events with the church of Christ:

1) 6000 Demons will be bound by the power of the Holy Spirit to allow the biggest harvest of souls ever for the church.
2) V-25-34: The woman with the issue of blood, healed talks about mighty healing, miracles, signs and wonders season the church of Christ is about to go through before the rapture.
3) V-22-23 and V-35 Jairus' daughter dead and resurrected is the parallel of the Rapture of the righteous. Check this out;
   - She was born the same year this woman came down to Jesus with the Issue of blood.V-25-42-43.
   - Now when Jesus died, after his resurrection, he appeared to people during 40 days. Remember, 40 jubilees or days or years represent 2000 years before He (body of Christ) be raptured. Genesis 7:17-18(Noah and the Ark), only 8 people saved (restoration).
   - Isaiah 46:9-13 Had a vision of the end time season before the rapture of the church...The anointing, double portion given to the Body of Christ to win Souls to the kingdom of GOD. Read also Numbers 14:34

THE MARCH OF PROPHECY: THE GRAPH

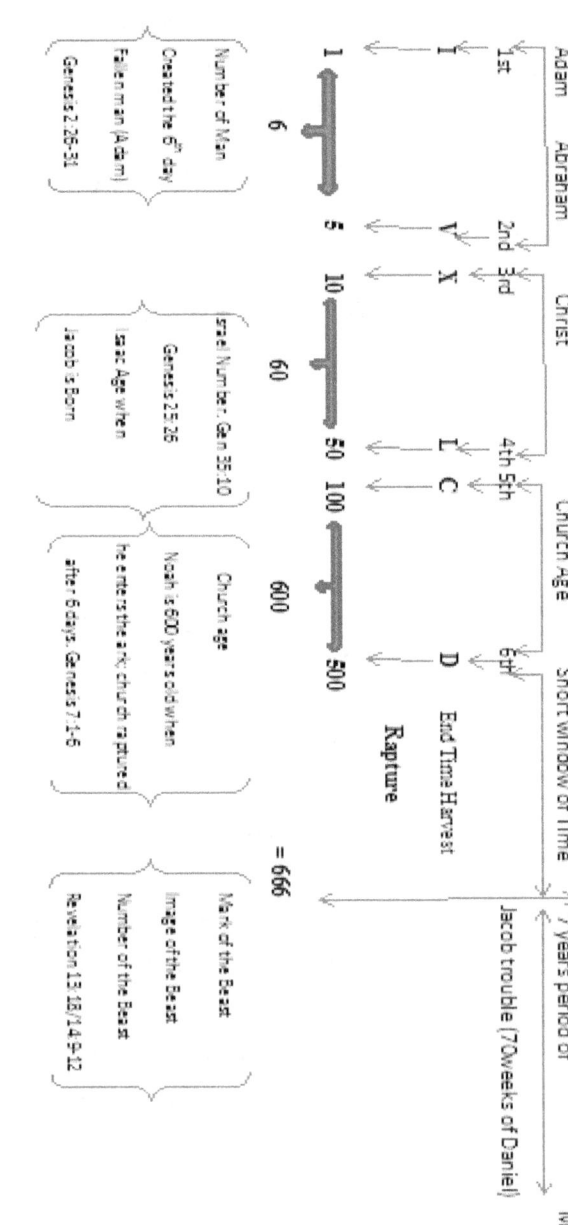

Adam	Abraham	Christ	Church Age	Short window of Time	Millennium
1st	2nd 3rd	4th 5th	6th		
I	V X	L C	D	End Time Harvest	
1	5	10 50 100	500	Rapture	
		60	600	7 years period of Jacob trouble (70 weeks of Daniel)	

Number of Man
- Created the 6th day
- Fallen man (Adam)
- Genesis 2:26-31
= **6**

Israel Number: Gen 35:10
- Genesis 25:26 Isaac Age when Jacob is Born
= **60**

Church age
- Noah is 600 years old when he enters the ark= church raptured after 6 days. Genesis 7:1-6
= **600**

Mark of the Beast
- Image of the Beast
- Number of the Beast
- Revelation 13:18 /14:9-12
= **666**

Let me blow your mind away: 2 Chronicles 3:8

* Do you see that 20 cubits+20 cubits= 40 cubits which represents 40 jubilees= 2000 years of the church age. Wow!

* The holy house (temple) was overlaid with 600 talents of fine gold= Church age... 2samuel 5:4

* Do you know that by the time God's house was finished, someone appeared (came), queen of Sheba (which means 7)...but let read 2 Chronicles 9:13... the total of Gold laid was now of 666 talents! That's why I prophecy by the time the church of Christ is ready into maturity, pure and build up and sanctified(Gold) the rapture takes place before the ministry of the beast 666 begins.

Footnotes: The three heads of Satan: 1) *The False prophet* - 2) *The Antichrist* - 3) *The Beast* (Revelation 15:2 & Revelation 16:13)

The Prophetic Calendar of GOD

HEBREW CALENDAR 2011 - 2012 (as an Example)

FOR THE JEWISH YEAR - AM 5772

--- A Hebrew Year of 12 months - 354 days ---
From September 29, 2011 ---Through--- September 16, 2012
--- 2012 is a Gregorian Leap-Year of 366 days - February has 29 days ---

This is the <u>BIBLICAL</u> ecclesiastical calendar, displaying days/dates which are according to the Word of God. The Roman calendar or Gregorian begins the year in winter (Northern Hemisphere). The bible Calendar begins in spring (Middle East). From the beginning of creation, from darkness came light; so the day begins and ends with Sunset (12H period: from 6 AM to 6 PM).

Hebrew Calendar

A New Calendar Day Begins At Sundown

#7 - Tishri 5772

Sun	Mon	Tue	Wed	Thu	Fri	Sat
				1	2	3
4	5	6	7	8	9	10
11	12	13	14	15	16	17
18	19	20	21	22	23	24
25	26	27	28	29	30	

On The <u>HEBREW'S</u> Calendar...
Rosh haShanah is: Thursday, 1 Tishri 5772
Yom Kippur is: Saturday, 10 Tishri 5772
Sukk'ot is: Thursday, 15 Tishri 5772
Sukk'ot ends: Wednesday, 21 Tishri 5772
Shemini Atzeret is: Thursday, 22 Tishri 5772
Simchat Torah is: Friday, 23 Tishri 5772

Gregorian Calendar

A New Calendar Day Begins At Midnight

Sept. - Oct. 2011

Sun	Mon	Tue	Wed	Thu	Fri	Sat
				29	30	1
2	3	4	5	6	7	8
9	10	11	12	13	14	15
16	17	18	19	20	21	22
23	24	25	26	27	28	

GREGORIAN Calendar: <u>AT SUNDOWN</u>...
Jewish New Year Begins: Wednesday, Sep. 28, 2011
Day Of Atonement Begins: Friday, Oct. 7, 2011
Tabernacles Begins: Wednesday, Oct. 12, 2011
Tabernacles Ends: Wednesday, Oct. 19, 2011
The 8th Day Begins: Wednesday, Oct. 19, 2011
Annual Torah Reading Cycle Ends: Fri, Oct. 21, 2011

#8 - Cheshvan 5772

Sun	Mon	Tue	Wed	Thu	Fri	Sat
						1
2	3	4	5	6	7	8
9	10	11	12	13	14	15
16	17	18	19	20	21	22
23	24	25	26	27	28	29

Oct. - Nov. 2011

Sun	Mon	Tue	Wed	Thu	Fri	Sat
						29
30	31	1	2	3	4	5
6	7	8	9	10	11	12
13	14	15	16	17	18	19
20	21	22	23	24	25	26

#9 - Kislev 5772

Sun	Mon	Tue	Wed	Thu	Fri	Sat
1	2	3	4	5	6	7
8	9	10	11	12	13	14
15	16	17	18	19	20	21
22	23	24	25	26	27	28
29	30					

Nov. - Dec. 2011

Sun	Mon	Tue	Wed	Thu	Fri	Sat
27	28	29	30	1	2	3
4	5	6	7	8	9	10
11	12	13	24	15	16	17
18	19	20	21	22	23	24
25	26					

On The **HEBREW'S** Calendar...
Chanukah Begins: Wednesday, 25 Kislev 5772

GREGORIAN Calendar: **AT SUNDOWN**...
Hanukkah Begins: Tuesday, December 20, 2011

#10 - Tevet 5772

Sun	Mon	Tue	Wed	Thu	Fri	Sat
		1	2	3	4	5
6	7	8	9	10	11	12
13	14	15	16	17	18	19
20	21	22	23	24	25	26
27	28	29				

Dec. 2011 - Jan. 2012

Sun	Mon	Tue	Wed	Thu	Fri	Sat
		27	28	29	30	31
1	2	3	4	5	6	7
8	9	10	11	12	13	14
15	16	17	18	19	20	21
22	23	24				

On The **HEBREW'S** Calendar...
Chanukah Ends: Wednesday, 2 Tevet 5772

GREGORIAN Calendar: **AT SUNDOWN**...
Hanukkah Ends: Wednesday, December 28, 2012

#11 - Shevat 5772

Sun	Mon	Tue	Wed	Thu	Fri	Sat
			1	2	3	4
5	6	7	8	9	10	11

Jan. - Feb. 2012

Sun	Mon	Tue	Wed	Thu	Fri	Sat
				25	26	27	28
29	30	31	1	2	3	4

12	13	14	15	16	17	18
19	20	21	22	23	24	25
26	27	28	29	30		

5	6	7	8	9	10	11
12	13	14	15	16	17	18
19	20	21	22	23		

#12 - Adar 5772

Sun	Mon	Tue	Wed	Thu	Fri	Sat
					1	2
3	4	5	6	7	8	9
10	11	12	13	**14**	15	16
17	18	19	20	21	22	23
24	25	26	27	28	29	

On The <u>HEBREW'S</u> Calendar...
Purim is: Thursday, 14 Adar 5772

Feb. - Mar. 2012

Sun	Mon	Tue	Wed	Thu	Fri	Sat
					24	25
26	27	28	29	1	2	3
4	5	6	7	**8**	9	10
11	12	13	14	15	16	17
18	19	20	21	22	23	

GREGORIAN Calendar: <u>AT SUNDOWN</u>...
Purim Begins: Wednesday, March 7, 2012

#1 - Nisan 5772

Sun	Mon	Tue	Wed	Thu	Fri	Sat
						1
2	3	4	5	6	7	8
9	10	11	12	13	**14**	**15**
16	**17**	**18**	**19**	**20**	**21**	22
23	24	25	26	27	28	29
30						

On The <u>HEBREW'S</u> Calendar...
Pesach is: Friday, 14 Nisan 5772
Chag ha Matzoh is: Saturday, 15 Nisan 5772
Yom ha Bikkurim is: Sunday, 16 Nisan 5772
Chag ha Matzoh Ends: Friday, 21 Nisan 5772

Mar. - Apr. 2012

Sun	Mon	Tue	Wed	Thu	Fri	Sat
						24
25	26	27	28	29	30	31
1	2	3	4	5	**6**	**7**
8	**9**	**10**	**11**	**12**	**13**	14
15	16	17	18	19	20	21
22						

GREGORIAN Calendar: <u>AT SUNDOWN</u>...
The Passover Begins: Thursday, April 5, 2012
Unleavened Bread Begins: Friday, April 6, 2012
Firstfruits Begins: Saturday, April 7, 2012
Unleavened Bread Ends: Friday, April 13, 2012

#2 - Iyar 5772

Sun	Mon	Tue	Wed	Thu	Fri	Sat
	1	2	3	4	5	6
7	8	9	10	11	12	13
14	15	16	17	18	19	20
21	22	23	24	25	26	27
28	29					

Apr. - May 2012

Sun	Mon	Tue	Wed	Thu	Fri	Sat
	23	24	25	26	27	28
29	30	1	2	3	4	5
6	7	8	9	10	11	12
13	14	15	16	17	18	19
20	21					

#3 - Sivan 5772

Sun	Mon	Tue	Wed	Thu	Fri	Sat
		1	2	3	4	5
6	7	8	9	10	11	12
13	14	15	16	17	18	19
20	21	22	23	24	25	26
27	28	29	30			

On The HEBREW'S Calendar...
Shavu'ot is: Sunday, 6 Sivan 5772

May - June 2012

Sun	Mon	Tue	Wed	Thu	Fri	Sat
		22	23	24	25	26
27	28	29	30	31	1	2
3	4	5	6	7	8	9
10	11	12	13	14	15	16
17	18	19	20			

GREGORIAN Calendar: AT SUNDOWN...
Pentecost Begins: Saturday, May 26, 2012

#4 - Tammuz 5772

Sun	Mon	Tue	Wed	Thu	Fri	Sat
				1	2	3
4	5	6	7	8	9	10
11	12	13	14	15	16	17
18	19	20	21	22	23	24
25	26	27	28	29		

June - July 2012

Sun	Mon	Tue	Wed	Thu	Fri	Sat
				21	22	23
24	25	26	27	28	29	30
1	2	3	4	5	6	7
8	9	10	11	12	13	14
15	16	17	18	19		

#5 - Av 5772

Sun	Mon	Tue	Wed	Thu	Fri	Sat
					1	2
3	4	5	6	7	8	**9**
10	11	12	13	14	15	16
17	18	19	20	21	22	23
24	25	26	27	28	29	30

On The HEBREW'S Calendar...
Tisha B'Av is: Saturday, 9 Av 5772

July - Aug. 2012

Sun	Mon	Tue	Wed	Thu	Fri	Sat
					20	21
22	23	24	25	26	27	**28**
29	30	31	1	2	3	4
5	6	7	8	9	10	11
12	13	14	15	16	17	18

GREGORIAN Calendar: AT SUNDOWN...
The 9th of Av Begins: Friday, July 27, 2012

#6 - Elul 5772

Sun	Mon	Tue	Wed	Thu	Fri	Sat
1	2	3	4	5	6	7
8	9	10	11	12	13	14

Aug. - Sept. 2012

Sun	Mon	Tue	Wed	Thu	Fri	Sat
19	20	21	22	23	24	25
26	27	28	29	30	31	1

15	16	17	18	19	20	21
22	23	24	25	26	27	28
29						

2	3	4	5	6	7	8
9	10	11	12	13	14	15
16						

I just felt impressed by the spirit of the Lord to add these Biblical Jewish Feasts.

1) Rosh Hashanah, The Feast of Trumpets, is the Jewish New Year

Rosh Hashanah Starts <u>At Sundown</u>...	Yom Teruah Hebrew Calendar Date...
Wed, Sep. 28, 2011	Thu, 1 Tishri 5772
Sun, Sep. 16, 2012	Mon, 1 Tishri 5773
Wed, Sep. 4, 2013	**Thu, 1 Tishri 5774**
Wed, Sep. 24, 2014	Thu, 1 Tishri 5775
Sun, Sep. 13, 2015	Mon, 1 Tishri 5776
Sun, Oct. 2, 2016	Mon, 1 Tishri 5777

2) Yom Kippur is The Day Of Atonement

The Day Of Atonement Starts <u>At Sundown</u>...	Yom Kippur Hebrew Calendar Date...
Fri, Oct. 7, 2011	Sat, 10 Tishri 5772
Tue, Sep. 25, 2012	Wed, 10 Tishri 5773
Fri, Sep. 13, 2013	**Sat, 10 Tishri 5774**
Fri, Oct. 3, 2014	Sat, 10 Tishri 5775
Tue, Sep. 22, 2015	Wed, 10 Tishri 5776
Tue, Oct. 11, 2016	Wed, 10 Tishri 5777

3) Sukk'ot is the 7-day-long Feast of Tabernacles

Tabernacles - Christ Jesus' Birthday Starts At Sundown...	Sukk'ot Hebrew Calendar Date...
Wed, Oct. 12, 2011	Thu, 15 Tishri 5772
Sun, Sep. 30, 2012	Mon, 15 Tishri 5773
Wed, Sep. 18, 2013	**Thu, 15 Tishri 5774**
Wed, Oct. 8, 2014	Thu, 15 Tishri 5775
Sun, Sep. 26, 2015	Mon, 15 Tishri 5776
Sun, Oct. 16, 2016	Mon, 15 Tishri 5777

4) Shemini Atzeret Is "The Assembly Of The Eighth Day"

The Last "Great" Day Starts At Sundown...	Shemini Atzeret Hebrew Calendar Date...
Wed, Oct. 19, 2011	Thu, 22 Tishri 5772
Sun, Oct. 7, 2012	Mon, 22 Tishri 5773
Wed, Sep. 25, 2013	**Thu, 22 Tishri 5774**
Wed, Oct. 15, 2014	Thu, 22 Tishri 5775
Sun, Oct. 4, 2015	Mon, 22 Tishri 5776
Sun, Oct. 23, 2016	Mon, 22 Tishri 5777

5) Simchat Torah means "Rejoicing in the Torah"

Simchat Torah Starts At Sundown...	Hebrew Calendar Date...
Thu, Oct. 20, 2011	Fri, 23 Tishri 5772
Mon, Oct. 8, 2012	Tue, 23 Tishri 5773
Thu, Sep. 26, 2013	**Fri, 23 Tishri 5774**
Thu, Oct. 16, 2014	Fri, 23 Tishri 5775
Mon, Oct. 5, 2015	Tue, 23 Tishri 5776
Mon, Oct. 24, 2016	Tue, 23 Tishri 5777

6) Hanukkah is The Festival of Lights.

Hanukkah Starts At Sundown...	Hebrew Calendar Date...
Tue, Dec. 20, 2011	Wed, 25 Kislev 5772
Sat, Dec. 8, 2012	Sun, 25 Kislev 5773
Wed, Nov. 27, 2013	Thu, 25 Kislev 5774
Tue, Dec. 16, 2014	Wed, 25 Kislev 5775
Sun, Dec. 6, 2015	Mon, 25 Kislev 5776
Sat, Dec. 24, 2016	Sun, 25 Kislev 5777

7) Purim celebrates Hebrew Esther's victory over anti-Semitic Haman.

Purim Starts At Sundown...	Hebrew Calendar Date...
Sat, Mar. 19, 2011	Sun, 14 Adar II 5771
Wed, Mar. 7, 2012	Thu, 14 Adar 5772
Sat, Feb. 23, 2013	Sun, 14 Adar 5773
Sat, Mar. 15, 2014	Sun, 14 Adar II 5774
Wed, Mar. 4, 2015	Thu, 14 Adar 5775
Wed, Mar. 23, 2016	Thu, 14 Adar II 5776
Sat, Mar. 11, 2017	Sun, 14 Adar 5777

8) The Passover is the day Jesus Christ was crucified.

The Passover Starts <u>At</u> <u>Sundown</u>	Pesach - Hebrew Calendar Date
Sun, Apr. 17, 2011	Mon, 14 Nisan 5771
Thu, Apr. 5, 2012	Fri, 14 Nisan 5772
Sun, Mar. 24, 2013	Mon, 14 Nisan 5773
Sun, Apr. 13, 2014	Mon, 14 Nisan 5774
Thu, Apr. 2, 2015	Fri, 14 Nisan 5775
Thu, Apr. 21, 2016	Fri, 14 Nisan 5776

<u>And, For Those Who Are Interested</u>:

Since <u>Easter</u> is capricious - and often occurs
a month *<u>BEFORE</u>* The <u>Passover</u>;

The Sunday *<u>FOLLOWING</u>* <u>Passover</u> is always the Sunday when one counts 50 days in order to determine the Sunday for <u>Pentecost</u>.
No matter *<u>WHEN</u>* <u>Easter</u> is celebrated!

The <u>Scriptures</u> teach that
Jesus Christ was <u>crucified</u> on The <u>Passover</u>...
Was <u>Resurrected</u> from the dead on the Feast of Firstfruits
(the Sunday *<u>AFTER</u>* <u>Passover</u>)...
And the Holy Spirit descended upon the apostles 50 days *<u>AFTER</u>*
that Sunday, on the Hebrew <u>High Holy Day</u> of <u>Pentecost</u>.

The Prophetic Alphabet - *the Chaldeans method*

According to the Chaldeans in the old world, they used a very prophetic and unique method based on the number of man (6).

The method is this: Using the alphabetic letters they attributed the first letter A the number 6...then on each other letter that follows the number 6 was added; so we come to this structure below:

A = 6

B= 12

C= 18

D= 24

F= 30

G= 36

H= 42

I= 48

J= 54

K= 60

L= 66

M= 72

N= 84

O= 90

P= 96

Q= 102

R= 108

S= 114

T= 120

U= 126

V= 132

W= 138

X= 144

Y= 150

Z= 156

Now let's calculate some names which when add together give the number

Of the beast: 666

| NECROMANCY | COMPUTER | STUBBORN |
| NEW YORK | | |

| UNRULY | SS NUMBER | INSANITY |
| US OF AMERICA | | |

| WITCHCRAFT | FFF | LUSTFUL |
| GORBATCHOV | | |

| MARK OF THE BEAST | VAN DEN BROEK | ILLUSION |
| KISSINGER | | |

BOOK OF THE DEAD   KATHOLISCHE   ⎡ VISA: VI= 6
Roman Numerical

SON OF SIN   CESAR NERON   ⎯ S= Stigma in
Greek whose value is 6

A PERDITION   VICRIUS FILII DEI ⎣ A = Babylonian
letter, whose value is 6

PONTIFEX MAXIMUS   DEUTSCHLAND

The ASCII Alphabet Characters

Symbol   **Decimal**
   Binary

A   65
   01000001

B		66
	01000010	
C		67
	01000011	
D		68
	01000100	
E		69
	01000101	
F		70
	01000110	
G		71
	01000111	
H		72
	01001000	
I		73
	01001001	
J		74
	01001010	
K		75
	01001011	
L		76
	01001100	

ETC...

2008, Year of Jubilee Revealed

A millennium is a full period of 1000 years. Now 2000 years ago, one man died for us on the cross his name is Jesus Christ.

According to the overview of the march of prophecy and after investigating the word of GOD, we noticed that **"1 day = 1000 years "2 Peter 3:8**

In 6 days the Lord GOD created the heavens and Earth, the invisible word and the visible one and rested on the 7th day.

6: represents the number of the creation, the number of man or of sin

7: represents the number of perfection of GOD, Fulfillment. In the previous chapter we found out that from ADAM to the Church today there is 6000 years. Genesis 5:1-32

Adam -----> Abraham: 2 days =2000 years

Abraham -----> Jesus: 2 days = 2000 years

Jesus ------> Church today: 2 days = 2000 years

Notes: *Genesis 11:26 and verses 31-32 It is good to get this, Terah Abram Father was 70 years old when he begat Abram.*

Back to our subject, we know that the church was born when Jesus Christ died on the cross, blood and water came out of him after being pierced by the roman soldier 2000 years ago. Back to our actual Gregorian calendar, when the world reached the year 2000, that was the beginning of the end of the Lease of this planet earth given by GOD to Men (Adam); that also mark the end of the 6 days.

A millennium is composed of years; for instance:

2000 is a millennium = 2 days + 1000

Now in the year 2008 for example, 8 represent the radical which determines the period or season. The number 8 symbolize, by interpretation of prophetic numbers (I will talk about that later in the book) new beginning, year of Restoration.

When Israel came out of captivity in Egypt, GOD commanded them to observe one thing: Leviticus 25:8-9/24 and that in that very year, the fiftieth year(50) was a jubilee celebrated and proclaimed throughout the land of Israel and more... read.

Notes: You will understand more why 2008 is the 50th year of Jubilee, season of blessings and that the next year 2009, season to possess the Land, sow seeds on the ground.

Every 50 years was declared a **year of Jubilee**; a year in which all debts were cancelled, everything they had lost or sold was restored to them: A year of Double portion.

This commandment to blow the trumpet in that particular year is and remain true today...Joel 2:15/19

When I examine deeper this number 8, several events are foreshadowed here:

- Gen 41:46-55 (v-50-54) Noah in the ark is saved along with his family(8people)
  new beginning. Read also Leviticus 12:3
- I believe according to the revelation I received from the Lord that from
  2000-2007, we have spent 7 years of plenty, breakthrough in any area of our society: Science, politic,

medical or Medicine, technology, inventions, religions, in the spiritual realm as well as physical realm.

One step deeper, Gen 41:50: unto Joseph were born two sons before the years of famine came…Joseph had the sons just at the end of the 7 years of plenty.

By the way, **Joseph** here is the type of the body of Christ or Jesus

Asenah his given wife: type of the world or Egypt.

1) The Firstborn Manasseh means the Lord made you forget all the toil, tragedy and pains of your father's house….Because Joseph has been faithful and came a long mighty way of persecution but kept his faith, the Lord shows him favor and goodness.

Here to paraphrase, it shows also all the breakthrough Jehovah GOD has bless us with: Technology, medicine, science,…to make us kind of forget our past of misery, failure and so forth, and have hope for a brighter future.

2) The second born Ephraim means for GOD has caused you to be fruitful in the land of your affliction…that's where 2008 shows up prophetically. Acts 2:17; Joel 2:23-30.

What GOD is saying is that HE himself will cause you to be fruitful, in other words it is not by mind, or by your strength or efforts but by his spirit says the Lord of Hosts.
"He causes you "*means also either you believe it or not, accept or refuse it, he will create or make that which he purposed to happen in your life without your help or even asking you.* My GOD I feel like preaching now! And that will produce a harvest.

Again, we see here that the land of thy affliction is for Joseph (even for us) Egypt (world) where he was falsely accused by

Potipherah's wife, put in jail as innocent; in other words those who afflicted you will remain alive and not die to see how GOD will bless you just like David said: Ps 23:5 **"Thou prepares a table before me in the presence of mine enemies, thou anointest my head with oil, my cup runneth over..."**

Number 50 is a prophetic number of jubilee, victory upon flesh, slavery, law and the enemy of our souls: Satan.
50 days after Jesus died; the power of the Holy Ghost came upon the disciples, Acts 1:8 Acts 2:17-18 Pentecost.
2008, new beginning, or we cannot talk about new if the thing is not first(1) therefore in 8 there is the number 1(first, new)on that note, we can say that a double portion of the Holy Spirit came down upon the church that year.

3) Now when Elijah had to be taken to heaven that very day (season of Jubilee) the bible reports that there were 50 sons of prophets standing on the other side of the river Jordan as witness. 2 kings 2:3/5/7.

Notes: *"In the economy of the universe, you are the currency and you spend that currency with your mind and operating in the spirit by Faith." Faith has the same value or currency than money; even more: with Faith you can buy anything from GOD for without faith no exchange or trade is made possible between you and heaven.*

    Prophet Christ

The 3 Major
Covenants of GOD's prophetic word

I will start by saying this: God greatest secrets are revealed in the covenant- through offering or sacrifice; the bible tells us that those who wait upon the Lord shall renew their strength. When you make a vow to GOD, you rest and stay still in whatever situation you find yourself in and He renews your strength, no work no effort...just wait and see!

The Covenant speaks louder than words look Genesis 4:9-10 (about blood covenant)

Now let me blow your mind:

Jehovah GOD can resist to your prayers, He can resist your worship or Praise **BUT** there is one thing **HE** cannot resist is the "<u>covenant offering</u>" you give with a cheerful heart.

Stay focus on what I'm about to reveal to you, this next step is *Awesome and Powerful.*

As I said earlier, there are 3 major covenants that the Lord revealed to me 7 years ago:

1) <u>**The Covenant of Bullock (Bull):**</u> **1 kings 18:22-23/32**

This covenant talks about deliverance, victory over your enemies. It breaks any resistance and strong holds in the spiritual realm. Judges 6:11-28/29-31. You see Elijah has made this covenant with the Most High GOD before the prophets of ball and won 100% by defeating the adversaries of the LORD by fire from above.

2) **The Covenant of Ram: Genesis 22:1-18**

Abraham, when asked by GOD to offer his only son Isaac went up on the mountain and when asked where the Lamb to be sacrificed is, He answered prophetically to Isaac: The Lord shall provide himself a lamb." *⁶ Abraham took the wood for the burnt offering and placed it on his son Isaac and he himself carried the fire and the knife. As the two of them went on together, ⁷ Isaac spoke up and said to his father Abraham, "Father?"*

"Yes, my son?" Abraham replied.

"The fire and wood are here," Isaac said, "but where is the lamb for the burnt offering?"

⁸ Abraham answered, "God himself will provide the lamb for the burnt offering, my son." And the two of them went on together.

⁹ When they reached the place God had told him about, Abraham built an altar there and arranged the wood on it. He bound his son Isaac and laid him on the altar, on top of the wood. ¹⁰ Then he reached out his hand and took the knife to slay his son. ¹¹ But the angel of the LORD called out to him from heaven, "Abraham! Abraham!"

"Here I am," he replied.

¹² "Do not lay a hand on the boy," he said. "Do not do anything to him. Now I know that you fear God, because you have not withheld from me your son, your only son."

¹³ Abraham looked up and there in a thicket he saw a ram caught by its horns. He went over and took the ram and sacrificed it as a burnt offering instead of his son. ¹⁴ So Abraham called that place The LORD Will Provide. And to this day it is said, "On the mountain of the LORD it will be provided."

Now understand this story: The reason why GOD did not give Abraham a Lamb is that Abraham could not by his righteousness sacrifice a lamb which means that he provided for us all a savior...God's plan was that **HE** will be the Lamb that will come to redeem us all from death and sin and, in other words GOD said to his servant: I have a covenant to make today with you as I promised (Genesis 17:1-8) to bless you beyond measure to become a Father for nations, and that Blessing passes through a test and sacrifice and the Ram is yours because today I ,the Lord establish you into your Destiny as promised, today you possess the land and the Lord GOD brought to him, a RAM.

The **_Ram_** here is the covenant of establishment, to reign and have total control, to possess the territory or land.

Horns: talks about destiny, your strength

Thicket: Talks about adversity, what holds you back and delay the process of blessing in your life. You see, so many things were delaying Abraham to enter into that covenant with Jehovah GOD and therefore, the Lord had to provoke Abraham faith to excel through this test, so that no more delay in his life. Notice that Abraham could have had a son earlier in his life but did not, God tried his patience for over 90 years and finally the time came for him to get the promise, after that, HE tried again his patience upon him with this act of obedience to see if Abraham finally understood the concept of that Mighty Blessing in which he was about to step in forever.

" [15] *The angel of the LORD called to Abraham from heaven a second time* [16] *and said, "I swear by myself, declares the LORD, that because you have done this and have not withheld your son, your only son,* [17] *I will surely bless you and make your descendants as numerous as the stars in the sky and as the sand on the seashore. Your descendants will take possession of the cities of their enemies,* [18] *and through your offspring all nations on earth will be blessed, because you have obeyed me." Gen 22:15-18.*

3) **_The Covenant of the Lamb:_** This covenant talks about fulfillment, it is made when expecting accomplishment of greatness in your life. The Lamb's blood covenant that declares and seals everything under GOD's property and possession. The Lamb here is **JESUS**. Isaiah 53

Glimpse on what is a VOW

Ecclesiastes 5:4

A vow is an order of what you want to manifest in your life. It is a contract, a conditional bargain with GOD.

It's also a persona l(solemn) promise to live and act in accordance with:

1) The rules of a religious order
2) God's words
3) Principles or decisions(promises)

God loves a man who keeps a vow. In fact a vow is a promise that you give and must respect or keep. 1 Samuel 1:9-11

It takes *faith* to stand before GOD and remain faithful (Full of Faith or Confidence) after you have made that vow: Let me say that *it takes your life*.

Example of Ananias and Sapphira Acts 5:1-11

Your vow is your spiritual Identification Card (S.I.C).Listen to this:

If you lose everything, all your ID's, passport, job title, resume, references, even your name…let me ask you this: what left of you is what? What do you think have left that tells others who you are? You have nothing else left except a question: *Do you do what you say you will do? Do you keep your promise, your VOW! My friend,* **you are your vow.**

There is no other currency in this world that you can spend with people than your words, your vows. A vow is a key to open GOD's goodness in your life.

Jacob understood the power of a vow; He changed his destiny, his future and fortune with a vow. Genesis 28:20-22

The right season to make a vow is when you are in the midst of hardship, where nothing is left except your faith and hope.

The bible says that a seed cannot bear fruit or produce by itself unless it dies first under the ground; buried first then, come alive again.

When you make a vow, you plant a seed in hard time, it makes your situation even harder because it takes a harder stone to break another one.(wow!) and **JESUS is that Harder stone you need to break the yoke in your life.**

In fact a vow is considered just like an offering, a sacrifice before GOD, therefore GOD will start to speak and reveal to you what in a normal situation would have not revealed it. Let's examine Judges 6:17-19, verse 25 is the result of Gideon's offering.

In Genesis 18:8-10 you see two things begin to happen when you make a vow:

1) GOD bless you, V-10
2) He reveals his plans and purpose to you, V-17-18 and V-21

I came to the conclusion that everything begins by a thought, which represents your desire, and then when you speak it out, it becomes a vow and the same vow brought before the altar becomes Sacrifice or offering.

During all my years in the prophetic ministry, almost 22 years now, I always do one thing; renew my vows with GOD by entering new covenants with HIM. When you make a vow to GOD, you make a covenant that silences your enemies because now HE holds your contract.

Notes: *Those who keep their covenant with the Most High GOD receive blessings in abundance, always: GOD has a covenant of Blessings with you, when you make a vow and keep it to execute it, when you become HIS.*

For example:

Covenant of Abundance & Peace (Deut 15:6-7; Deut 30:9; Ps 92:12; Is 41:18; Gal 3:29; Eph 2:14)

Covenant of Assurance & Victory (Eze 34:16; John 14:18; Heb 13:6-8; Rom 8:28; Malachi 3:6)

Covenant of Authority & Power (Gen 1:27-28; Gen 9:2; Luke 10:19; Eph 1:19/22-23; Isa 54:17)

Covenant of Deliverance & Healing (Exo 3:8; Isa 10:27; Ps 68:20; Isa 43:13; Dan 3:17-18;

Covenant of Miracles & Salvation (Eph 2:8-9; Acts 4:12; Exo 14:14 /27-29; John 3:16; 2Cor 5:17)

Covenant of Prosperity & Wisdom (Joshua 1:8; 3John 1:2;2 Cor 1:20; **Lev 25:21**;*Lev 26:9)...etc.*

THE LAW OF BECOMING

Exodus 7:1

Who are you? You may have thought you knew the answer to that question! But you did not...

Don't tell me your name, that's what you are called, not who you are. Don't even give me your title or Alias, because those are just attributed to you.

Until you know who you are, you will not understand where you belong. Once you understand this then you knows why you are here on Earth, the purpose of you being born in that family, that city, that nation.

In Exodus 3:13-14 (read). GOD says *"I AM".* In those two words resides the revelation of our true nature, our real identity in the Lord. GOD placed you into this world not to wait around for HIM to put things together in your hands; but for you to declare the *"I Am"* yourself.

You were sent here on earth by the Great *"I AM"* and in you that *"I AM"* is the state of your entire existence: **_There is divinity in YOU._**

If you examine the scripture closer, that's exactly what Lucifer told Eve in the Garden, but twisted that in the wrong way of thinking, pushing her to sin against GOD's word.

The truth is that Adam was created with that divinity in him, the Great "I AM" was his state of existence. Man is the only creature with the power to create and shape his world; to bring things into existence by first thinking about it, then manifesting it: **calling things that are not as though they are.** *Roman 4:17*

All things begin in the mind. Who else has the power to create what did not exist before? GOD of course. When you declare your *"I AM"* nature, you are claiming your divine birthright and step into your role as GOD's proxy in this world; you discover your purpose reason: which is to walk in divinity and authority! Exodus 3:1-2. Listen By becoming aware of the Spirit of GOD within you, you become that spirit; what really happen is that The Spirit of GOD takes control of your personality, your body: Your hands become His hands, your mind, your eyes, become His…your body become His Temple…*Yours ..Become His.* Hallelujah!

One of my top revelations is when the LORD told me one day**: Don't choose to be…Chose to become who I called you to BE.** Here how I break it down for you:

BE: Is stable…you are (present time)

COME: Is Movement. Going from A to B. You enter another level. Most of the time we are and because we are and declare so, and accept it, we cannot ***BECOME.***

Becoming talks about your future, about your destiny. And because you are becoming, GOD will begin to send people on your way to prepare you and give you what you need for your destiny.

See the scripture in **1 Samuel 10:1-9.**

Remember GOD never gives you anything that you do not need. What does a doctor do? He practices.

People in life become (more proficient) because they practice. If a doctor does not practice his medical knowledge, He will lose for sure his license to practice.

Life is exactly the same way: understanding and acting on the word of GOD will guarantee you stability and success and prosperity in life.

Some people miss the fun in life because they hate practicing: With enough practice, what you are looking for *will find you*.

In Luke 15:11-32 we read the story of the Prodigal son who <u>became</u> someone else.

1) He is seduced in his father's house to temptation of moving away, just like EVE, in the garden or like Judas among his Brothers (John 17:12).
2) The country of Death attracts him in Verse 13. And only a dead person can confuse light and darkness; life and death.
3) He counts on his own strength to solve the problem in time of famine and sorrows.
4) He thinks that he is wiser than his father or anybody else; and before He know it, he is confused Verse 16. Now let's read verse 17:
5) He comes to himself…which means that HE WAS NOT HIMSELF WHILE DOING AND MAKING THOSE DECISIONS. He got eyes but could not see, the ability and the power but incapable of reaction; he could feel but not discern, could hear but not understand; could touch, but not possess. Someone else, another spirit was doing it.

Finally he wakes up and now, surrenders to the Holy Spirit: His live is given back to him… better, He **BECOMES** a brand new person whom the father is proud of.

Note:
You may be caught into a traffic jam in your life, but I dare you to magnify the Lord thy GOD, I will surely manifest his goodness to you.

Prophet Christ

The coming *F*inancial *E*arthquakes

First of all, let me tell you this:

From this page forward, I begin to unfold some major prophecies that the Lord GOD gave me beginning in the year 2008.

*"**The purpose of Prophecy IS NOT to scare you but to prepare you**"*

We are in the beginning of one of the greatest crises that this world has ever experienced. It is an economic crisis that will shake the entire world. This crisis is not control by any government; no leader or human power is behind it….I should say: Satan has no control, *BUT* **GOD** alone!

The Lord GOD has always used his prophets to warm his people about future judgments.

In Amos 3:7 it reads: **"Surely the Lord GOD will do nothing, but he revealeth his secret unto his servants the prophets."**

In the Old Testament times and times again GOD used Noah to warn of a coming flood.

- ✓ Abraham and Lot his nephew of the future destruction of Sodom and Gomorrah.
- ✓ Joseph warned and prepared the people for seven (7) years of famine in Egypt.
- ✓ Elijah, the prophet of GOD was directed to warn of a coming famine in Samaria.

GOD is speaking, who is listening???

In the New Testament, GOD has spoken in many ways:

Mat 24:4-14; Luke 17:26-32; 2 Tim 3"1-11; Acts 11:27-30; in this last scripture the Lord used Agabus (prophet from Jerusalem) to warn the believers in Antioch about a famine which was coming upon the entire world. Now notice the response to the prophetic word:

***"Immediately upon hearing it, they acted upon it."*Verse 29**

The people did not try to reason with GOD or question him as to why he was sending judgment, they simply believed and acted.

<u>Notes:</u> One of Satan major strategies for attacking your finances is to cause you to keep from giving to the Lord; he keeps your eyes on your financial needs and problems until you do not look up to Jesus for his supernatural Provision.

Prophet Christ

Satan will attack your finances and cause you to doubt God's care and provision, instead of trusting him. He wants to keep your eyes on the large sum of money you owe, on your bank account, on your paycheck; on your bills; on depending on men…He wants to keep your spirit focus on your LACK: Lack of Money, lack of Clothes, Lack of Nice car, lack of Furniture… *But I stop by here to tell you "the devil is a liar and he is defeated, under our feet in Jesus Name".*

<u>The time has come for GOD's children to get their eyes off the natural and embrace the supernatural season in which GOD is in total Control</u>. Deuteronomy 8:3-10

In his relationship with Israel, GOD planed they would experience this supernatural provision during their 40 years in the wilderness.

He supernaturally led them by a pillar of cloud by day and a pillar of fire by night; He rained Manna from heaven, caused water to gush out of rocks and met all of their needs.

Their clothes did not wear out, nor did their feet swell for 40 years. When they entered the promise land they were not poor or sickly. Psalms 105:37

The disobedient generation died in the wilderness, but GOD brought a new generation to possess his promises: **Deuteronomy 8:7-9; Deuteronomy 15:4-5**

The Lord GOD has placed prophets within the body of Christ; they are part of the fivefold ministry (Ephesian 4:11) and serve a specific purpose. GOD uses prophets to give spiritual focus and direction, to reveal his plans and purpose and to warn and prepare the body of Christ for whatever coming ahead.

The word of GOD is clear: "**The Lord GOD will do nothing unless HE reveals first his secrets to his servants, the prophets.**" Amos 3:3

Notes: *Deuteronomy 8:1 "The covenant anointing begins with obedience: First you obey, next you go forth, multiply and possess the land."*

Prophet Christ

5 Major Crises (2008-2014)

2 Chronicles 20:20 *"... Believe in the Lord your GOD, so shall ye be established; believe his prophets, so shall ye prosper."*

1) <u>**A Crisis of Change:**</u>

   The Lord GOD revealed to me that there will be such dramatic changes in society that people would find it difficult to cope with.
   Changes around the globe, weather, climate, politics, financial, cultural... changes that will affect nations and people(Strong cold seasons, avalanche of snows and increase of strong winds and tornadoes...these are coming before the big earthquake).

2) <u>**A Crisis in Family:**</u>

   Rebellion will be everywhere, breakdown of moral standards. We have seen this already with children murdering children, violence committed in schools, campuses; abortion and divorce rate being increased at the speed of light; sexual transmitted diseases.

   God is not pleased with the sexual lifestyle that gay man and women live today. There is fornication and adultery, incest and sexual abuse everywhere and people around are powerless, allowing the devil to take control of what we were supposed to control at the first place.
   Half of couples who live together are not married; GOD is not pleased with any of it.

3) **A Crisis in the Church:**

God revealed that there will be a shaking and great shifting in the church structure; that its *structure* will change and the true body of Christ will emerge in a new form.
You will witness the increase of persecution around the world; a new leadership within the Five (5) fold ministry will rise, denying God's principles and the Doctrines of Prophets and Apostles which is the foundation of the Gospel.
But at the same time, tradition of *Man-made* will be broken in the church and the Lord GOD will be the great and true Shepherd that will feed the flocks with Holiness and true and sound doctrines. Ezekiel 34:1-16

4) **A Crisis of Satanic Confrontation:**

GOD revealed that the body of Christ will face satanic confrontations that will be greater than any time in history, for the time for the prophecies spoken by the prophets in the Old Testament has come. There will be a time of intensified spiritual warfare, where demons will manifest themselves and directly confronting GOD's children.
We see these things happening in our society and culture via multimedia, TV programs and Movies...Today there is NO channel on TV where you tune and not find Vampires presence, Wolf, Violence and killings....***This is it my brethren, this is the time!***
Spiritual doors have been already opened; we have reach the limit of non-return, limit of prohibited frontier by the Most High GOD and violated our own privacy by allowing the kingdom of darkness to control us and lead us instead of turning to the "strong Tower, our Refuge and Strength" JESUS CHRIST.

5) A Great Financial Crisis:

The Lord GOD revealed that this is the last of the five crises to come and we have been already into it since 2008 but the pic of the iceberg is coming out of the water NOW. The dark clouds are coming and the manifestation of the black horse of the apocalypse in revelation 6, v5-6 can be seen in both natural and spiritual worlds.

__I come here to prophecy again: When this worldwide financial crisis hits America and around (we do not see the hidden part of the Iceberg yet), our monetary system will collapse and, it will be sudden!__

The consequence thereof is one monetary world system **(Euro)** and one world government **(New World Order)** led by the European Union. A **One World Leader** has been already chosen and awaiting in shadow for the prophetic timing to come out and lead this world to its final days.

Now at this stage, allow me here to release 3 specific prophecies:

a) Inflation will accelerate astronomically
b) The scarcity of food will be prevalent; Gas price will continue to rise like gunshot …Famine will be a common occurrence not only in Africa but in the entire world. There will be world manipulation for food; some nations will have more foods that others and this will create revolts and calamities everywhere.

C) Russia joining forces with the Middle East will attack Israel trying to take over the Oil and Wealth therein. The Lord GOD said to the angel you can pour judgment upon the earth, but when you see those who represent the oil and wine (Blood of Jesus and sealing of the Holy Spirit), do not harm them.

Back to Crisis 3:

Psalms 122:1 says" *I was glad when they said unto me, let us go into the house of the Lord."*

In the Church you will see a division coming within the body of Christ. There are going to be sideline compromisers who think that they can speak in tongues one minute and drink cocktails and wine and smoke cigarettes next minute.

People who think they can have one foot in the world and the other foot in the church. The Lord GOD said: I'm going to separate them; they will no longer be sideline compromisers. In Matthew 11:12 we read: *"And from the days of John the Baptist until now the kingdom of heaven suffered violence and violent take it by force."*

<u>Notes</u>: *Cycles of prosperity:*

Give to GOD - → *Receive Supernatural provision + increase .2 Chronicles 31:9-10*

Supernatural transfer of Wealth: *Job 27:16-17; Proverbs 13:22; Proverbs 28:8*

"The Law of the Harvest is that you reap in proportion of what you sow" 2 Corinthians 9:6-9

The Name BARAK in Prophecy

PART I:

Proverbs 14:35 *"A true witness delivereth souls, but a deceitful witness speaketh lies."*

Coming to the spiritual understanding of the prophecy, let us examine these facts:

Regarding the actual president of the United States of America, Barack Obama, it is amazingly shocking for some to consider this truth, but let's see:

Fact 1: Reading **Judges 4:8** where for the first time in the Bible, that name is mention, we emphasis here that Barack was born **on 8/4.**

Fact2: Reading **Judges 12:4**: *[4] Jephthah then called together the men of Gilead and fought against Ephraim. The Gileadites struck them down because the Ephraimites had said, "You Gileadites are renegades from Ephraim and Manasseh."*

He was elected on **11/4** and his Social Security codename is Renegade.

Fact 3: Judges 4 contains assign that Barack would need to invite Hilary to the battlefield as did Barak with judge and prophetess Deborah. As Secretary of State, Hilary wields more power than she would have had as Vice President of the USA.

Fact 4: Name of Blasphemy (False Prophet) Luke 10:18; Revelation13:1

"And I said unto them, I beheld Satan as lightning falling from the heavens"

These words are originally in Aramaic language; the most ancient and primitive form of Hebrew.

In Hebrew Lightning means **Baw-Rawk** or **Baw-Rak** or **Baraq**, is a primitive root; to lighten; cast forth or a flashing sword. Isaiah 14:12-19.

Verse 14: Heights = Heavens which translated in Hebrew gives **Bam-Maw** or **Bamah;** to be high; an elevation; high place; wave... In the Hebrew language the letter **Waw** or **Vau** is the 6th letter of the Hebrew alphabet translated as a "U" or "O".

It is used as a conjunction to join concepts together. Now Lightning Falling from the Heights or Heavens will be: *Baraq "O" Bam-Maw* or *Baraq "U" Bam-Maw.*

Back to Luke 10:18 what the Lord Jesus was saying, translated in the English language will be: *"And he said to them, I beheld (saw) Satan as Barak "O"Bama .   Revelation 13:1*

PART II: *John 16:25; 2 Peter 1:21*

DANIEL 7 REVEALED: *End Time Prophetic Chapter and WW III*

There are **7** prophecies in Daniel that occur before **WWIII** breaks out, and the election of Barack Obama fulfills the 6th of these prophecies.

The Four (4) great BEASTS: which come out of the sea and their importance.

V-3-V-17: Coming up the sea and the Earth because *the beast symbolizes both a nation and the Leader of that Nation*. Please Very important to understand this before I go deeper into revelations.

In verse 7, Daniel the prophet describes the New World Order: **The TEN (10) Horns.**

They are leaders of the world's nations of today and they will all support the **NWO**

(New World Order).

In Verse 8, the little horn is the antichrist, I should say the one who bears the "name of Blasphemy"; he comes out of the midst of the Ten(10) world's leaders, from **NWO**.

Reading Daniel 7:8... When the three (3) kings are plucked up that refer to **WWIII**. Now the verse says this:"...before whom 3 of the first horns were plucked up..."in other words WWIII occurs before the antichrist makes his public appearance; His identity will be revealed or released only by the second half of the great tribulation.

Verse 8: Four (4) Horns and Verse 9.

Four (4) Attributes of Almighty GOD and in verse 10 Daniel the prophet uses the word Thousands 4 times. This is the third (3rd) consecutive verse where the number 4 is used. There are four (4) extremely important numbers in the End Time Prophetic Season to remember: *4; 7; 12 and 28.*

Back in Chapter 4, Daniel the prophet uses the number Seven (7) 4 times and in Chapter 7, he uses the number Four (4), at least 7 times.

Let me break down the revelation for you as the Holy Spirit gives me wisdom:

There are 4 Winds that blow on the sea.

There are 4 Beasts

There are 4 Horns

There are 4 Heads of the Leopard

There are 4 Wings on the Leopard

There are three "4" in three consecutives verses of Daniel and if you look Chapter 7 , it is divided into four (4) sections of 7 verses each: Just like the weeks in the month.

7 Days in Each Week

4 Weeks in a month.

In Chapter 7 and verse 4 we see the End Time Prophecy unfold.

The Lion with Eagle's wings: England and the wings that are broken off symbolized *her colonies*: particularly the *USA*.

Verse 5: Another Beast: **The BEAR** who is **Russia**- Stood up on one side means it has leftward political learning. The three (3) Ribs in the mouth indicate that it *devours much flesh or it maintains control over its neighbors.*

Russia is currently led by a premier minister whose name is **Dmitry Medvedev**, known as the **BEAR** of Russia. Coincidence you think? *Not at all.*

In Verse 6: The next Beast out of the sea is the **Leopard or America** and its leader *Barack Obama.*

The 4th Beast: with 10 Horns representing the Rebirth of the Roman Empire, the Little horn is the antichrist rising in the midst of the European union.

Now listen to this: The leopard has a skin which is both black and/or white /yellow, that symbolizes the racial makeup of America (Multicultural nation).

Verse 7-8: The Beast with 10 Horns: The Eagle, the 10 beast nations (system of Apostasy).

AMERICA IN PROPHECY

a) The Four (4) wings are the 4 military branches of our government:

ARMY – NAVY – AIR FORCE – MARINES

b) The Four (4) heads are the 4 branches of our government:

SENATE – WHITE HOUSE – PRESIDENT – SUPREME COURT.

And dominion indicates that power is given to the USA as <u>world's lone superpower</u>, for a time and a season of times. No other nation in the world fulfills this prophecy of Daniel 7 like America.

Now the Leopard was elected to lead America. Barack Obama and that the 4 wings and 4 heads, when add together gives you 44. Obama is the 44th president of the United States of America. Wow!

The 3 nations plucked out

BEAR (Russia)   **LION** (England)   **Leopard** (America) this means that these nations are involved in the coming WWIII instigated by the antichrist behind the scene.

According to Judges 12:4 Barack Obama will provoke Russia. B.O is called the leopard in chapter 7 and in chapter 11:36-37, the last King of the south and also the last president of United States of America. ***Daniel look forward towards the future end time prophecy and the apostle John looks backward and the two visions come into fusion of this present season. 7 Times in the bible: 2 times in Daniel and 5 times in Revelations.***

Secrets Unsealed

Daniel 9: 70 weeks of Daniel= 490 years

Daniel 7:25 Great tribulation

Time=1 year

Times= 2 years   Revelations14:5   ½ times= half year =3 and ½ x2   42months= 3and ½ years   1260 days= 3 and ½ years;

After 483 years the Messiah is cut off and Jerusalem is destroyed (62 Weeks)

John 16:1-3 Prophecy of end time / Jesus Christ

THE SPIRIT OF THE ancient EMPIRES

IN *AMERICA*

In every major world Empire, according to biblical prophecy, there is evidence of a domination spirit that influences the leaders and governments of this world.

In Daniel 10, two (2) of these spirits are identified as "Prince of Persia" and The Prince of Greece" Daniel 10: 13-20.

The name: Prince" here does not talk about earthly ruler, but *strong principality spirit*.

Revelations 9:13-15

It is clear that global armies which are under the influence of evil spirits will conduct the prophetic wars of the future in this end time season. Revelations 16:13-14

Let's see their influence in USA and open your eyes on what is going on really in our land:

A) The spirit of Babylon:

The Babylonian empire was considered for the large numbers of astrologers, stargazers and occult activities. Daniel 3 and 6. Many years ago now, America has experienced a revival of occultism. It began with innocent TV programs showing witches and witchcrafts then developed to popular programs where people claimed to be able to contact the dead (forbidden in scriptures: Leviticus 19:26/31 and Leviticus 18:20-24).

Students are involved with role playing fantasy games such as Dragons & Demons, Dominion Rules, Dying Earth, Dragon Ball, Science fiction (SyFy and company), Horror movies, superhero, etc... That introduces them to occult concepts, paranormal activities and occult science such as: Ritual Magic, servant of the Light school of Occult science, Vampires culture, dragons tattoo and ancient evil symbols tattoo, without understanding they are lost.

<< Police statistics show that after investigating, they begin to realize that many of the crimes they investigate have occult origins. >>

B) **The spirit of Media-Persia:**

The Medes and Persians overthrew the Babylonians regime. They were known for passing **_laws_**. Once the law is set, it could not be reversed (See Daniel 6:15; Esther 3:7-14).
In America, the Supreme Court has made three (3) major decisions that have influenced and changed the destiny in this great nation in a *negative way*.
1) In 1963, they removed prayer & Bible reading from public schools
2) In 1973, they legalized abortion on demand.
3) In 2003, they began to permit more freedom to the homosexual community.

In Daniel's time he felt that the law of GOD was Superior to the law of Medes & Persians and he was jailed for that; like today many ministers of the Gospel of Jesus Christ are jailed when they protest in any form of speech or action.

C) The spirit of Greece:

The Greeks sought after wisdom and in the process they began to listen to every form of teachings and philosophy and different beliefs of many religions in the world.

In those days they worshiped over 30 gods. Actually there were 37 gods & goddesses altogether, such as Zeus, a mythological god who was popular among many others like Eros, Aphrodite, Hercules, Dionysus, Apollo and others...

In acts 17:23, when Paul the apostle preached in Athens on Mars Hill, he observed one monument dedicated to the "UNKNOWN god". *They culture was noted for their tolerance which has become the politically correct word for America.*

Tolerance for every religion, every belief and *alternative lifestyle* (Homosexual, lesbians, etc...).

D) The spirit of Rome:

America has many parallels to the Roman Empire; let's go through each of them prophetically:
- Rome had a senate, America also have one.
- Rome had a Hill Capitolina, America has Capitol Hill
- Rome had one man as the head (Caesar), America has one head (President)
- Rome had Roman & Greek architectures; America (Washington) has roman & Greek Buildings.
- Rome emblem was an eagle, America emblem is an eagle
- Rome had the world's greatest military, so does America have

- Rome occupied the Middle East region, so does America
- Rome dealt with Palestine, America with Israel
- Rome loved the chariots race, America loves the NASCAR race
- Rome loved Stadiums sports, America main sports are in Big Stadiums.
- Rome felt from immorality, America is being corrupted by immorality and following the downhill road.

Conclusion:
The Babylonian empire extremely rich with gold, made loans to their neighbor the Medes & Persia; then they could not repay every 3 years a double interest. Finally they plotted an invasion against Babylon.
Daniel the Prophet reports that Belshazzar the king, during a huge party in the banquet hall was overthrown. Daniel 5:1-30/31.
Darius the Median became king...after that Cyrus the Persian.

Cyrus the king overtook Babylon and initiated the Media-Persia Empire which made loans to Greece and the same story happened: The Greeks could not pay back then, plotted an invasion or war against the Media-Persia Empire and we know the story, Alexander the Great took over after and became the greatest Empire of all time.

The growing burden of debt by Roman government was too much and began to heat up in Palestine (Israel) in 66 A.D; The Roman armies marched their legions into Israel and smote the Jewish rebels who were weary (tired) of high taxation.

The revolt failed and in 70 A.D, the temple of Jerusalem and the walls of the city were set to flame and destroyed by **Titus.** Read Daniel 2:31-35/44-45; Revelations 12 & 13:1-3

Notes: The danger of powerful Empires when their debt become uncontrollable and lead to invasion, wars are initiated, money shifts hands and new Empires are forged who control the credit and Cash flow(Money Supply) just like the Federal Reserve Banks. **In the same way that Rome moved from a producing Empire to a purchasing Empire, so is America following the same path to destruction. The word Republic comes from the Latin Republica= public affairs, when the people revolt and gain independence.**

The War of GOG and MAGOG in Prophecy

In this great chapter, I will go step by step with biblical scriptures and historical evidences to settle the march of prophecy concerning what we know as the GOG & MAGOG War. Get ready to be blown away!

Ezekiel 38:1-6 and Revelation 20:7-9

After the great flood, Noah and his 3 sons repopulated the entire world;
We have: **HAM, SHEM** and **JAPHETH**; so in one sense we are all related cousins.
In Genesis 10, the bible lists the 70 original tribal groups that we call "*Table of Nations*." Now to understand Ezekiel 38 and 39 we need to identify GOG and MAGOG.

MAGOG: was one of the sons of Japheth, actually he was the 2nd son .**Genesis 10:2**
He founded the magogians or magogites who lived in the region of Caucasus mountains in Greek they are called Scythians (according to Joseph Flavius and Herodotus, Greeks historian): They are descendants of Magog.
They drank the blood of the first enemy they killed and carried the heads of the victims to their chiefs. They scalped their enemies and used the scalps as "Napkins"
It is reported also that they used the skins of their victims to cover their quivers (a case full of arrows).They did practice blood brotherhood by drinking each other's blood mixed with wine.
Now in Greek mythology, the Scythians descended from scythes; the youngest of the 3 sons of Hercules, from sleeping with a half viper and half woman.

They are very nomadic tribes from Russian steppes, a fertile area of Ukraine North of the Black sea: they are **_Russians_**.

They colonized Media, Parthia, Persia, Central Asia and as far as the Chinese borders.
In Arabic, the *Great Wall of China* is called: **"The wall of Al Magog"** built to keep out the invading armies from MAGOG, Soviet Union or Russia: 2000 square miles.

GOG: is the leader or King of MAGOG. Now Ezekiel the prophet back then could not prophesy against Russia, because Russia did not exist yet or I should say existed under another name: MAGOG.
GOG is the prince of Rosh, Meshech and Tubal read in Amos 7:1 (also taken from the Masoretic text, 9th century). And it says this: "Thus the Lord showed me. And behold a swarm of locusts were coming, and behold one of the young devastating locusts was GOG, the king" (earlier translation of the old testament into Greek, known as the Septuagint).
But compare with Proverbs 30:27 "the locusts have no King" meaning that in Amos 7:1 it is not about natural locusts as insect, but rather an army of People...also read Revelation 9:3-11

Notes: Angel of Abyss: **Hebrew = Abaddon**
Greek = Apollyon

Abaddon in Hebrew means ruin, destruction read Job 31:12. Place of destruction, the abyss, realm of the dead: Job 26:6 and Proverbs 15:11 (Sheol).

Now in revelations he is personified as Apollyon, the angel-prince of hell, the minister of death and author of "HAVOC" on earth. From Greek Apollyon, to Latin Exterminatus it means Destroyer or Terminator.

Now we have GOG, ruler of the land of MAGOG (Russia), king of the locusts, leader of the Russian led in invasion of Israel and then Associated with the angel-prince of hell: Lucifer.

The question now should be: who are the other members of that army?

I am glad you ask, so let's examine the word of GOD. They prophesied by their ancient or old tribal names: *Ezekiel 38:3-6* here we go deeper.

Meshech-Tubal- Persia-Cush and Put; Gomer- Beth Togarmah (One thing in common, guess what? *They are all Muslim tribes.*

Notes: I would like to point out here some revelations about where we all came from.

Out of the 3 sons of Noah: Shem – Ham – Japheth

Shem gave **the Semitic**

Ham gave **the Hamitic or African**

Japheth gave **the Indo-European**

Semite - a member of a group of Semitic-speaking peoples of the Middle East and northern Africa.

Caucasian, White, White person - a member of the Caucasoid race

Babylonian - an inhabitant of ancient Babylon

Chaldaean, Chaldean, Chaldee - an inhabitant of ancient Chaldea

Assyrian - an inhabitant of ancient Assyria

Phoenician - a member of an ancient Semitic people who dominated trade in the first millennium B.C.

Arab, Arabian - a member of a Semitic people originally from the Arabian peninsula and surrounding territories who speaks Arabic and who inhabits much of the Middle East and northern Africa

Aramaean, Aramean - a member of one of a group of Semitic peoples inhabiting Aram and parts of Mesopotamia from the 11th to the 8th century BC

Canaanite - a member of an ancient Semitic people who occupied Canaan before it was conquered by the Israelites.

Back to the tribal names:

1. **Meshech**: the 6th son of Japheth. He was the ancestor of Mushki of the Assyrians and Muschoi of the Greek; Inhabiting Phrygia in northern *Anatolia* (actual Turkey). He links the Muschkoi with the Muschkovi or Muschkovich which is the ancient name of Russia.

2. **Tubal**: The 5th son of Japheth. A city brother of Meshech (eastern Anatolia), regrouping all the countries of the old Soviet Union before.

3. **Persia**: Includes descendants of *Elam*, the 1st son of Shem which is now called **IRAN**. Iran was known as Persia until it changed its name in 1935 unto "New Persian". A leading ally in the Ezekiel list and present major exporter of" Islamic fundamentalism" all over the world and America. So Persia is **IRAN/IRAQ.**

4. **Cush:** Referred to a piece of land lying around the Nile, in the south of Egypt and translated in the bible as **Ethiopia or Nubia or Black Africa.**

    a. There are dozen strategic materials essential to the modern military in the world and available only in two (2) regions of the globe: **Russia and Africa.**

    b. **Zaire (now Democratic Republic of Congo)** has 95% of the world's known reserves of Chromium, 52% of Cobalt, 53% of Manganese, 64% of Vanadium or Uranium and 86% of Platinum. Zaire is called the "Persian Gulf of Minerals".

    c. **South Africa and Russia** control over 90% of the world's supply of Platinum, 94% of Manganese, 90% of Chrome, 95% of Vanadium or Uranium. Importing only Bauxite, Barium and Fluoride. Ethiopia and Egypt are parts of Central and South Africa.

5. **Put:** The 3rd son of Ham; founder of Libya. The Inhabitants were called Putites; it is associated with North Africa populated by *the Berbers*. Here the composition: **Libya – Mauritania – Maghreb – Algeria – Tunisia – Morocco**. Read Genesis 10:6-7.

6. **Gomer:** In the Babylonian Talmud (Sacred Text Archive), the father of Ashkenaz is rendered "**Germania**" Hosea 1:3. He is the ancestor of Germanic Tribes that defeated Roman Empire and populated the Western Europe, Rhine and Danube valleys. The ***French*** came from the *German Frank Tribe* and the ***English*** came from the *German Anglo-Saxon tribe.* Read Genesis 10:3; 1Chronicles 1:6 and Jeremiah 51:27.

7. **Togarmah:** Son of Gomer. The Assyrians called them Til-Garimmu, a name derived from the Hittite City Tegarama or Gauraema presently known as Gurun: 70 miles west of Mylayta. But Destroyed by Sennacherib in 695 B.C.

   Togarmah = Armenians = Turkey and Turkestan, Asia, Kazakhstan, Turkmenistan, Uzbekistan, Tadzhikistan, kyrgzitan; to joint their Islamic brothers in the MAGOG war. They are independent republics, Islamic and have nuclear weapons.

   Notes: The antichrist is not one man but a system of apostasy and rebellion. Daniel 7:25. How such thing could happen in the church/The 13th apostle Constantine (Mother Helen) changed the Sabbath.. Matthew 5:17-18 now the question is: who did change the Law?
   In 135 A.D **Emperor Adrian** Prohibited the keeping of the Sabbath day, and Sabbath was changed to Sunday and Passover to Easter Sunday. But GOD Said: "I AM The Lord, I changeth not".

The Kingdom of the Antichrist

All hell is loose and the Kingdom of Satan is in great progress and formation. Let us list here prophetically those nations awaiting the time to openly declare their allegiance to the antichrist.

Syria	**Egypt**	**Iraq**
Turkey	**Pakistan**	**Iran**
Lebanon	**Libya**	**Jordan**
Saudi Arabia	**Kuwait**	**Afghanistan**

GOD is shaking the whole world: First of all the shaking is natural and economic with lots of disasters everywhere in the world.

Secondly: war and political disasters with use of nuclear weapon and atomic bombs.

Notes: The false Messiah is the false prophet .Read John 5:43

Now there are two secrets that make America a Strong Nation *and if those two are broken, America will not survive.*

1) Civil liberty: Freedom from the King
2) Religious Liberty: Freedom from a Pope

But also there is a prophetic implication with that: Just like the people of the New Testament, when time came to choose for themselves <u>*a king*</u> between Jesus Christ of Nazareth and Rome (Caesar), remember what they said:

"We have NO KING but Caesar" Wow!!

GOD and the Ministry of Angels

I came to a breakthrough in my spirit about some scriptures in the bible talking about the angels, the clouds, winds, spirits, flame of fire, smoke, chariots of fire, horsemen of fire and much more...

To start this teaching or before I share with you these deep revelations, let us read some scriptures for you to grasp the essence: 2 King 2:11

We see Elijah raptured in chariots of fire with the horsemen of fire by a whirlwind which translated means "storm of Clouds". It seems that GOD sent one of his chariots to take the Prophet Elijah to Heaven that day.

Throughout the Bible we read scriptures that let us understand the meaning of chariots and thick clouds of fire and smoke...let's examine Psalms 68:17-18; Habakkuk 3:8; Exodus 19:16-18.

The angels of the Lord are chariots of fire: Jeremiah 4:13, in charge of catching away the saints or righteous from the earth to Heaven.

Habakkuk 3:8; Hebrews 2:3 refer to angelic deliverance; Colossians 3:4; Romans 8:17-18; Colossians 1:27.

Back to 2 kings 2:4-5

The very fact that Elijah the Prophet of GOD and the sons of the prophets knew the exact day of Elijah's rapture <u>could indicate that GOD may Reveal the Time and Season of the Rapture of the Church to his Servants, the Prophets before it Happens</u>. O, Praise the LORD!

The fact that Elisha stayed on earth and received a double portion of the anointing would seem to indicate that Elisha represents or profiles the 144,000 Jewish of Revelation 7.

Let us compare Mat 17:1-5 and 2 kings 2:1-13, **this is the end time generation for GOD.**

Reading the word in Hebrews 1:7, the angels of the Lord are made spirits or winds...

2 chronicles 5:13-14; Psalms 105:39 = psalms 104:3-4 = Hebrews 1:7 = 2 kings 6:17 = exodus 13:21-22 = Acts 1:9-12... Now let us read Numbers 9:15 with Mat 17:1-3; when we see Peter asking to dress the tents as he understood the cloud of glory just as we did in Numbers 9:15 or Isaiah 6:1-7.

What is an Angel?

The word angel is thought to be derived from the Greek word "Angelos" which means "messenger". In Christian, Muslim, Jewish and other theologies an angel can be one who acts as a messenger, attendant or agent of God.

Throughout the bible it is generally seen that the will of God is usually imparted or carried out by angels.

Angels are spirits without bodies, who possess superior intelligence, gigantic strength, and surpassing holiness.

Angels are composed of ethereal matter, thus allowing them to take on whichever physical form best suits their immediate needs.

They enjoy an intimate relationship to God as His special adopted children, contemplating, loving, and praising Him in heaven. Some of them are frequently sent as messengers to men from on high. Angels are the essence of love and joy and stem from the Heart of God.

Angels are countless in their number, and flock around the Universe in their millions. Angels are dedicated to serve the needs of all free will entities so that you may experience the same level of unconditional love as they do. Each Angel carries out its assigned task without any hint of hesitation as they take great joy and pleasure in offering their Loving Wisdom and Guidance. Everyone has Angels around them constantly, without exception, and they are eager and excited at the opportunity to communicate with you.

In Christian religion and theology, a fallen angel is often classed as a devil, like Satan himself; whereas a guardian angel is classed as a human guide or protector. Angels are commonly represented by a figure with wings and wearing a long white robe. They are also sometimes depicted wearing halos which emanate from the angels' head in a glorious wreath of light, serving as a symbol of divine wisdom. Angels do not die or age, they are immortal, created by God and existing since the Creation. Generally they are accepted as being the guardians of souls. Although angels are generally divine, they have been shown to be fallible and prone to sin, particularly pride. One of the most notable examples of this being Satan and his fallen army. ***Ezekiel 28:1-19***

Angels can take on a variety of different forms. In Ezekiel 1:16-21, Isaiah 6:1-3, and throughout the book of Revelation they are described as taking on not only the appearance of men but many fantastical forms. A notable example was the angel who took on the appearance of a burning bush. The image of an angel with wings tends to symbolize the spiritual nature of the being. The purpose of the wings being to allow the angel to travel through the ether as well as being a symbol of divine authority.

Angels are everywhere and you can ask for Angels to assist you with anything you wish. There is no limit! In fact, if no Angel is available for a particular task, an Angel is created as an answer to your wish or prayer, just for you! However, the love that they have is just as immeasurable.

Remember - Angels are bound by the laws of Free Will. Therefore, they cannot assist us in our lives unless we ask them too. So, don't forget to ask!

- Angels appear to us with many forms and shapes.

A Spirit Guide is also a free will entity, but has evolved over what you would consider to be a long time. They are part of a group consciousness of beings that have evolved beyond form into beings of pure light and essence. Although Angelic in nature, Spirit Guides are a free will entity and therefore choose their path of further growth. Spirit Guides are master teachers and are able to travel and navigate through many, many levels of existence. They are here to Guide and teach when you are willing to listen. They are always communicating to you through your thoughts, music, your environment, wherever they need to be in order to get your attention.

Everyone has at least one Guardian Angel, and sometimes two or three. A Guardian Angel is a being that is dedicated to serve and to help you throughout your lifetime. However, the relationship is somewhat deeper than that. Your Guardian Angel was created out of the same essence that makes up your soul. It could be said to be a higher, or essence aspect of yourself. Your Guardian Angel isn't essentially separate from you; it has absolute and unequivocal dedication to you and travels with you on every journey that you as a free will entity choose to make. Your Guardian Angel makes an agreement with your soul to assist it in completing any task it has decided to undertake. This is the reason why Angels have been known to make miraculous rescues from accidents. If a soul has decided to remain focused on the Earth Plane for a given length of time, an Angel will assist in getting someone out of trouble who's 'time is not up'. Angels and their miracles are God's way of remaining anonymous.

An Angel is complete, unified and centered within the Heart of the Divine at all times. An Angel does not question or contemplate itself, it simply is. In being itself, it is a bundle of God's ever present love and grace. An Angel has been created to serve, love, hold and support those to who it is assigned, and those who ask for Angelic support. Angels are to be found in every corner of the Universe, and in their millions! If you could see Angels with the naked eye, you would be amazed at just how populated the Earth really is. Have you ever felt a breath of cool air brush along your cheek when alone somewhere? That might very well have been an Angel moving aside as you walked into an Angel conference, quite unaware!

Angels of GOD Hearken to the Voice of GOD himself:

Ministering spirits

Hebrews 1:3-14; psalms 103:20-22

In this section of the Book, I would like to make a transition and talk about the division of Angels in Heaven. But first of all let me tell you this: Demons **are not angels** but coming from the pre-adamic world. And that Subject will be developed in our next chapters.

Ephesian 6:10

Five (5) Divisions of Dark angels or falling angels:

1- Spirits
2- Principalities
3- Powers of darkness (Exocias = Authorities)
4- Rulers of darkness (when man are possess by demonic power)
5- Spiritual hosts (Wreaked Spirits)

Just as you can see, there is also:

Five (5) Divisions of GOD's angels:

1- **Seraphim :** Isaiah 6:1

They have six (6) wings each and say to each other: Holy, Holy, Holy is the Lord...

The Seraphim's are the angels responsible of caring the Glory of GOD , in other words, When we talk about the Glory of GOD , we talk also about the presence of those Angels, fulfilling they duty.

The Seraphim without question they are the closest in all of heaven to the very throne of God, and their primary function is to circle the incomprehensibly beautiful throne in perpetual adoration of the Lord. This is a task that is not nearly as monotonous as it may seem to mortals, given the nature of the angels (who have perfect powers of concentration) and the delight that such an honor actually brings to the spirits.

The Seraphim are almost always identified with fire-not the burning, painful flames and heat of hell, but the healing flame of Love. They are literally living flames. The intensity of their adoration and pure Love of God pure out of them as a flawless reflection of the Divine Love that emanates from the Lord. Like the rising sun, each angel radiates such light that even the other Holy Beings, the Cherubim and the Thrones cannot look upon them.

According to the Bible, each Seraph has six wings. In the Old Testament Book of Isaiah (6:1-3) he writes "...I saw the Lord sitting upon a throne, high and lifted up; and his train filled the temple. Above him stood the Seraphim; each had six wings: with two he covered his face, and with two he covered his feet, and with two he flew." In the Book of Revelation (4:8) is another possible reference: "And the four living creatures, each of them with six wings, are full of eyes all around and within, and day and night they never cease to sing 'Holy, holy, holy, is the Lord God Almighty who was and is and is to come

2- **The Cherubim:**
   Ezekiel 1:5
   The word Cherub: Are the angels who look like men; they have four (4) Faces and Four (4) wings.
   The sole of their feet were like the sole of a calf's foot, because they are in the presence of GOD, walking up and Down before the throne of GOD; just like Lucifer did walk before. The Cherub is connected with worship; they are in the ministry of the Holy Spirit V-11-12. The cherubim's are moved by the Holy Spirit or GOD's presence.
   Genesis 3:22-24. The Cherubim have always been much more active on Earth, protecting all God's creations. No other Order works harder (only the Powers are their equals in relentless devotion to duty). If humans knew just how much the Cherubim have done for them, they would have praised the Living GOD even more.
   The Cherubim are also given the task of maintaining the records of heaven and seeing to the details necessary to keep order in the Heavenly Host.

3- **Zoë:** Greek word which mean: Living Creatures or as read in revelation 4:1, they are the beasts. Interesting to notice here that they are quiet similar to Seraphim and Cherubim; also connected to GOD's presence V-6-8.Ezekiel 1:5-24.

4- **Archangel:** 1Thessalonians 4:16. They announce the coming of the Lord. In the beginning of time, we had:

* *Gabriel*: as the messenger of GOD. Luke 1:19

* ***Michael***: General of the Army of the Lord (In charge of Warfare) Daniel 10:13

* ***Lucifer***: falling archangel in charge of Worship Ezekiel 28:1-19; revelation 12:7-9

Notice that Gabriel is also involve in the warfare, but not as much as Michael who also received the command from GOD Himself to protect Israel at all time.

Remember that the totality of the Host of Heaven has the supernatural power from GOD to do mighty miracles, and even deliver battles in heavenly places as well as on earth.

5- **Common Angels:** Acts 1: 10. They look or have the appearance of men. These angels are connected with the church, the body of Christ, and each Christian in GOD's family.
Hebrews 1:14
The angels of GOD are mention in the bible more than 300 times and always refer to their ministry among men and their services rendered to the only KING of universe: YHVH.

At this time, let us examine fourteen (14) truth or facts about angels:

- ➢ *They are Wise: 2 Samuel 14:20. They know everything that happens on Earth. See V14*
- ➢ *Powerful: Revelation 18:1*
- ➢ *Obedient: Psalms 103:20*
- ➢ *They have their Own will: Isaiah 14:12 they have a free-will to make choices or decisions.*
- ➢ *They never Sleep: Revelation 4:8 but notice that contrary to demons who seek rest Matthew 12:45*

- ➤ *They Can Eat: Genesis 18:8 (only when they take the man (Flesh) appearance)*
- ➤ *They Appear and Disappear: Hebrews 13:2*
- ➤ *They Speak: 1Corinthians 13:1*
- ➤ *They Strengthen us in times of troubles: Luke 22:43, they care and encourage us.*
- ➤ *They Protect the Saints: Psalms 34:7-9*
- ➤ *They are involved in giving us spiritual sight and revelations about GOD's word. They can help us plan our lives for success, they assist us: Acts 5:19*
- ➤ *They Bring answer to our prayers, Acts 10:1-6*
- ➤ *We don't have to pray or worship them: Colossians 2:18*
- ➤ *They are without number: Daniel 7:9-10; Psalms 68;17*

Some will talk about the seven (7) heavens, the seven (7) orders of angels and bring you to a gulf with no return possible, but I am here to tell you NOT TO BELIEVE OR ACCEPT SUCH Lies from the pit of hell: **The devil is a Liar**. There are three (3), and only 3 Heavens and above as mention are the categories of angels in Heaven.

THE *PRE*-ADAMIC WORLD

{Please take time to read all the scriptures I will mention here, then for sure you will come to a breakthrough in the spirit of understanding the wisdom of GOD}

This is one of the great Chapters in this Prophetic book where we all go for a spiritual journey in the Spirit of the LORD our GOD.

The Bible says: **The Spirit of Prophecy is Jesus Christ and Jesus Christ IS the Spirit of Prophecy.**

As I'm about to bring you one of the most tremendous revelation of all time, I ask you to ask the Holy Spirit to keep you in prayer, and total understanding of each stapes. Are you ready?! So let's begin the journey!

The Anointing is released through the knowledge of GOD's word. The degree of your anointing depends on the prophetic knowledge given to you by GOD himself through the Holy Spirit. <u>The WORD works only if you know it.</u> Lack of knowledge brings death to the Soul.

<u>**Genesis 1**</u>

<u>**The Beginning**</u>

<u>[1] In the beginning God created the heavens and the earth. [2] Now the earth was formless and empty, darkness was over the surface of the deep, and the Spirit of God was hovering over the waters.</u>

We see here that these two verses talk about CREATION.

GOD started by creation Heavens, then Earth; The Invisible World with the angelic being (angels) then after that, the Visible World (with human being).

Now to understand this section let's translate the two verses in Hebrew:

V-1: Bereshit Bara Elohim at hashamayim meaning: In the beginning GOD created the heavens…

Beginning =Bara which means, brought out of nothing it's also a dateless past.

Bara is to create out of nothing.

Elohim = is the plural of GOD (Trinity) Father-Son-Holy Spirit

Eloi= singular form of GOD which interpreted means *Father only* (Mark 15:34) without the rest of the trinity: The Son and the Holy Spirit.

Shamayim= is the plural of Heaven(s)

> *Genesis 1:8 is about the First Heaven*
>
> *Ephesians 6:13-15 is about the second Heaven*
>
> *2 Corinthians 12:1-4 is about the Third Heaven*

V-2: we see the verb in the past:' WAS" translated in means "BECAME"

Now at this point we understand that there must be a first stage where this Earth is perfect, before "Becoming" without form. BUT we all know that GOD is perfection, whatever He creates is PERFECT, **the million dollars question** comes out now :What really happened to this "Perfect Earth with form to become , all of the sudden "Without Form and Void"???

Deuteronomy 32:4 *God's work is perfect*

Isaiah 45:18 *Never in Vain or Chaos*

Ecclesiastes 3:11 *Everything beautiful*

Psalms 18:30-32 *God's way is perfect…* **Hallelujah! So what happened then!?**

Back to Verse 2: to become, it must be first because the *law of becoming* is always influence by the *law of First*. The Holy Spirit brought me back in the beginning and the past and throughout the all scriptures to finally reveal to me the mystery of many generations before us, now came to light. Amen!

As we continue, I just feel in my spirit to drop this down here, **Genesis 1** is not the creation, only the verses 1 and 2 are about Creation. Wow!

The rest of the Chapter is , and get this: **"RESTORATION"** The Almighty GOD had to Restore what had been destroyed, voided and brought to chaos by an "EVENT" which I am about to reveal to all of you. Follow me closer now… That's why the scripture talks about restoration in our lives because the enemy has destroyed; stolen ad killed some part or something from us.

Billions of years I should say exist between Verse 1 and Verse 2 of Genesis chapter 1.And between V-1 and V-2 the Fall of Lucifer took place, remember *we are here in a Spiritual journey back in time, way before Adam and Eve were created; we are in the* **Pre-Adamic World.**

When we read JOB 9:1-15 we understand that it all about the Pre-adamic world and what happen during GOD's anger. *Notice verses 5-8, and then read Genesis 1:2… doesn't sound like the same event here?? Of course YES it does and we will read more of that.*

During that time past, the war between GOD and Lucifer began, his rebellion against the almighty One, supported by his fellows: the fallen angels. The Earth that GOD created in perfection was destroyed because of his rebellion and great sins (keep reading as I open your spiritual eyes to see clear, by the power of the Holy Ghost).

All my life , even before I became a servant of GOD and called to be one of his prophets, I heard ministers of the gospel saying all kind of irregularity and lies about Satan rebellion and how he fall from grace….and believe it. Years later now, my eyes are open to the true word of revelation and prophetic anointing that breaks the yoke of ignorance and slavery.

Let us now examine what **REALLY** happened in Heaven and what <u>are</u> the reasons of GOD punishment and judgment upon one of the most powerful archangel ever created: Lucifer and the World thereof.

The prophet Ezekiel, living in his time, had the mighty revelation of the pre-adamic world and what really happen; being in the days of the LORD in spirit he saw therefore wrote these for us today to grasp and "know the truth and the truth shall set us free."

Ezekiel 28: 1-19

[1] The word of the LORD came to me: [2] "Son of man, say to the ruler of Tyre, 'this is what the Sovereign LORD says:

"'In the pride of your heart
you say, "I am a god;
I sit on the throne of a god
in the heart of the seas."
But you are a mere mortal and not a god,
though you think you are as wise as a god.
[3] Are you wiser than Daniel?
Is no secret hidden from you?

⁴ By your wisdom and understanding
you have gained wealth for yourself
and amassed gold and silver
in your treasuries.
⁵ By your great skill in trading
you have increased your wealth,
and because of your wealth
your heart has grown proud.

⁶ "'Therefore this is what the Sovereign LORD says:

"'Because you think you are wise,
as wise as a god,
⁷ I am going to bring foreigners against you,
the most ruthless of nations;
they will draw their swords against your beauty and wisdom
and pierce your shining splendor.
⁸ They will bring you down to the pit,
and you will die a violent death
in the heart of the seas.
⁹ Will you then say, "I am a god,"
in the presence of those who kill you?
You will be but a mortal, not a god,
in the hands of those who slay you.
¹⁰ You will die the death of the uncircumcised
at the hands of foreigners.

I have spoken, declares the Sovereign LORD.'"

¹¹ The word of the LORD came to me: ¹² "Son of man, take up a lament concerning the king of Tyre and say to him: 'This is what the Sovereign LORD says:

"'You were the seal of perfection,
full of wisdom and perfect in beauty.

¹³ You were in Eden,
the garden of God;
every precious stone adorned you:
carnelian, chrysolite and emerald,
topaz, onyx and jasper,
lapis lazuli, turquoise and beryl.
Your settings and mountings were made of gold;
on the day you were created they were prepared.
¹⁴ You were anointed as a guardian cherub,
for so I ordained you.
You were on the holy mount of God;
you walked among the fiery stones.
¹⁵ You were blameless in your ways
from the day you were created
till wickedness was found in you.
¹⁶ Through your widespread trade
you were filled with violence,
and you sinned.
So I drove you in disgrace from the mount of God,
and I expelled you, guardian cherub,
from among the fiery stones.
¹⁷ Your heart became proud
on account of your beauty,
and you corrupted your wisdom
because of your splendor.
So I threw you to the earth;
I made a spectacle of you before kings.
¹⁸ By your many sins and dishonest trade
you have desecrated your sanctuaries.
So I made a fire come out from you,
and it consumed you,
and I reduced you to ashes on the ground
in the sight of all who were watching.

*19 All the nations who knew you
are appalled at you;
you have come to a horrible end
and will be no more.'"*

Well, as you read by yourself, you got the revelation, don't you?! Here two more scriptures to help you breakthrough into prophetic revelation: Isaiah 24:1-6 which paints Genesis 1:2; **Isaiah 14:12-20; Jeremiah 4:23-31 also talks about that particular moment of genesis 1:2...**

Now Satan, fall into many sins against GOD, but we can see how the Lord was so patient with him even though HE knew for so long what Lucifer was doing behind his back...He waited patiently then spoke the judgment against him: **Listen to what he said: I will set <u>my throne</u> on high...why? Because he was under, also going up and down, from heaven to earth to exercise his duties: <u>Priest</u>, <u>King</u>, <u>worshipper</u>, <u>holder of Light</u>**. Now we see, he was a king, has a throne, has sanctuaries, and therefore was a Priest. He was to give the worship of the earth to GOD and take GOD's love and give it to the earth: Ezekiel 28:15-16

He was to give GOD's word to the nations thereof. If He was able to corrupt third of angels He must be powerful... Now we know why Jesus has to come, why the blood needed to be shade. It's not by mind, nor by power, but by my Spirit says the Lord. We don't only need angel to protect us, but above all we need the blood of Jesus, the Holy Spirit to guide us in spirit and truth.

**"You were blameless in your ways
from the day you were created
till wickedness was found in you.
16 Through your widespread trade you were filled with violence,
and you sinned.**

"Notice, that not only he became arrogant, but also did trade with souls of men, trade of any kind of nature... Let me speak with my own words now:

What the Lord GOD did , was to place Lucifer on earth as his Proxy, to be the priest, governor, chief intendant of GOD's creation, at that time they were Inhabitants on earth as we can see, it's about kings, therefore kingdoms, therefore people or subjects; there were cities built read carefully Jeremiah 4:20-26/29, also Isaiah 24:1-6. All these events happened in the time past, even before Adam and Eve were created .The verbs are all in the past tense, describing Genesis 1:2 nothing else and the chaos thereof. The prophets grasped the move of the Spirit of GOD as He revealed himself to them with mighty visions.

Here is the prophetic interpretation as the Spirit of GOD unfolds it on me:

Lucifer is cast out of heaven, down to earth, with his companions and the effect or impact once touching the ground is so powerful and heavy that a big hole is created from where he fall, creating therefore a _PIT_. The bible says that fires came out of GOD and devour him, reducing him into ashes: Ezekiel 28:18-19. You see the Lord GOD did not create _Hell_ for you and me, but by the falling of the "star" Lucifer and company on the ground.

... And I reduced you to ashes on the ground
in the sight of all who were watching.
[19] All the nations who knew you
are appalled at you;
you have come to a horrible end
and will be no more.'"

As a spirit, Lucifer cannot die, so his companion and the inhabitants thereof; the bible does not give us a clear knowledge on how they looked like those pre-adamic inhabitants,

but by the spirit of revelation we know that they were not created on GOD's image at all. How?, ***because the only time GOD will say and do it is in Genesis 1:26***.

The Lord executed the judgment and destroyed the pre –adamic world...***There was the First flood that destroyed that world. Noah's flood was the second and last.*** Now we have the explanation why in Genesis 1:2 it says:" ... *and the Spirit of GOD moved upon the face of the waters*". but Jeremiah 4:27 says" ...*Yet will I not make a full end*".

Now remember, Lucifer and companion are in the PIT, the earth is destroyed... after a while, GOD decide to bring ORDER back, RESTORATION to the creation from his chaotic picture: That is where Genesis 1: verse 3 and down comes in the picture, not as creation verses, but restoration verses. Wow!

Let's prove it!

In Hebrew there are two (2) verbs used for creation, but only one verb in English to use. That's where confusion in interpretation of the prophetic comes.

As I said before, BARA means to create out of nothing, something...that is use for genesis 1: verse 1.

The other word is ASA: ***which means to make, mold or form, take from something and create something else out of it.*** Ok don't stone me yet, I'm just starting! Amen.

Now, back to Genesis 1: verse 3 and down, we have the ***"let there be"*** or ***"let"*** syntax which many of us (servants) did not breakthrough in revelation.

In English, the "Let" is not a verb, neither a word (declaration) of creation, but a word of permission, allowing things to be, or become…etc… Got it?! Good.

So when GOD says: let there be light, it is because, upon his judgment to the nations and Lucifer, the light did not shine, nor the stars give their light…see by yourself in **JOB 9:6-9**

Jeremiah 4:23-27…

In conclusion of this "Let", we see that Genesis 1 is a chapter all by itself, mixed with creation sections and restoration sections (verses), O Lord open the eyes of our hearts to see you clearly. ***But rest ensured that definitively, Genesis is the book of beginning.***

> Here I come to break the generation ignorance of beliefs that said that demons are fallen angels or else…The inhabitants that were destroyed suddenly in the pre-adamic world by flood, but yet the flesh only, not the spirit: **they are the Demons of today and for centuries, hunting and possessing people with evil**.

Note:

Again, let me point it out: *Demons are earthly bound being* and *Angels are Heavenly bound being.*

A pre-historic Elephant or if we wish, a pre-adamic Elephant was found in Siberia **frozen with food in his mouth**. Historians say, only a sudden destruction could have caused an Elephant to die while eating such way, and with the climate changes, got frozen.

In JOB 38:1-7 GOD ask job, where were you JOB? When I did all these things? Verse 25-30…in Psalms 104:4-9 .In Verse 5, GOD set the foundations of the Earth back then. Read verse 7: Flood rebuked and waters began to separate: Genesis 1:8

In Job 38:7 the morning Stars are the angels of GOD presents during the creation and the restoration of the Earth; they did shout for joy in the sight of all this events taking place. *I could go on and on with lots of scriptures but won't have enough space in my book.*

When the Lord GOD says in Genesis 1:26

"^{26} Then God said, "Let us make mankind in our image, in our likeness, so that they may rule over the fish in the sea and the birds in the sky, over the livestock and all the wild animals, and over all the creatures that move along the ground." Lucifer is already in the PIT with the fallen angels, waiting for another chance to go up.

Then we have the story of Adam and Eve, created; but watch carefully what the Lord recommends them to do and why?

" ^{28} God blessed them and said to them, "Be fruitful and increase in number; fill the earth **and subdue it**. Rule over the fish in the sea and the birds in the sky and over every living creature that moves on the ground."

The Lord God will not use "Subdue the Earth" in vain, if there was no danger. You subdue something when you know someone else may take it over, therefore you have to control it, put banderies all around what is yours.

It was GOD's way of telling Adam, there is someone here before you, and if you don't pay attention, what I gave you he will still it from you. And that is exactly what happens.

From his hiding prison, Lucifer chose the most crafted animal among all, the serpent; comes out of the **_PIT_** as a spirit deprived of his power and strength but, not of his ability to move and operate as a spirit. He then possesses the serpent, giving it the ability to speak and deceive EVE. By doing so with success, He then regain strength and power and, gathering again his companion, try to get back to heaven. Only by this time, the Almighty GOD of Universe has placed a seal between heavens, and HIS Throne. Lucifer does not have access any more into GOD's glorious presence nor his kingdom. And till he comes across the second heaven and gets refrain right there. **And by decree of the Great I AM**, he now has been granted (punished) the _exiled place of the second heaven_ as his habitation. Now the bible comes in Ephesians 6:12-17 and says this truth:

"*[12] For our struggle is not against flesh and blood, but against the rulers, against the authorities, against the powers of this dark world and against the spiritual forces of evil in the heavenly realms. [13] Therefore put on the full armor of God, so that when the day of evil comes, you may be able to stand your ground, and after you have done everything, to stand. [14] Stand firm then, with the belt of truth buckled around your waist, with the breastplate of righteousness in place, [15] and with your feet fitted with the readiness that comes from the gospel of peace. [16] In addition to all this, take up the shield of faith, with which you can extinguish all the flaming arrows of the evil one. [17] Take the helmet of salvation and the sword of the Spirit, which is the word of God.*"

Well, from now you may be shaking and scratching your head saying: this is way too much information and revelation I ever got in my life! That's right, when the Spirit of prophecy and revelation comes upon you; there is a shift, then breakthrough in Jesus name.

The Curse after the *FALL* and the *5* Underworlds

Genesis 2:1-14

But in Verse 4, it says: [4] this is the account (or these are the generations) of the heavens and the earth when they were created, when the LORD God made the earth and the heavens.

Here we will talk about what happen next after the account of previous chapters.

The spirit of God will reveal us mysteries in this chapter to break the curtain of ignorance once for all and enlighten our understanding in Christ Jesus.

Let's start with **Adam** account:

Verse 7: [7] Then the LORD God formed a man from the dust of the ground and breathed into his nostrils the breath of life, and the man became a living being.

Notice first, that man is formed from the **dust**, why not the ground? Well, because after GOD's judgment upon Lucifer, HE decided to make man according to His nature, to have dominion, not only on the beast, the Fowls, but be also above Lucifer who was on the Ground already at that time. The Lord GOD could have chosen the ground, but did not instead took the Dust which is the evaporation of the Ground particles flying over.

For me, the ground is already curse even before Adam and Eve got there, because of Lucifer; but the curse is executed thereafter they both sin.

Notice also that **ASA** (to make or form from something) here is the verb in Hebrew used to form man from the dust, not **Bara** (to create out of nothing) as for the beginning of creation or **Panach** in Hebrew meaning to build.

Ish = Man and **Ishach** = woman=she-man

Let's go a little more ahead in chapter 5, verse 1-2

We see the bible says: [1]This is the book of the generations of Adam. In the day that God created man, in the likeness of God made he him;

[2]Male and female created he them; and blessed them, and called their name Adam, in the day when they were created. (King James Version)

Notice that the bible says, he created man, then says: GOD made he him.

Verse 2 says: male and female, but we know that man was created or formed and that woman was taken out of man. Right? So the prophetic interpretation is that in ADAM, **were** both man and woman. The woman is the hidden part of the man, the invisible part of him, now manifest before his eye. It's like the man could see a part of him he did not know existed before. And GOD does it majestically by giving man a deep sleep to unveil the other part of himself: the Woman= taking from the man. Wo-Man, out of man. From this understanding, we see why the man Adam will say: This is now bone of my bones, and flesh of my flesh: she shall be called Woman, because she was taken out of Man.

Again, we see the Lord God here performing by forming out of something existent, a miracle of creation: A rib from the man, becoming a wo-man. Genesis 2:22

Now, the wo-man will be named later on by the man Adam as Eve as the mother of all living: Genesis 3:20.

Now in 1 John 2:14-16 we see what happen when the woman was tempted by the serpent and why was she tempted, according to Paul the apostle, this is the path to fall: **[14] I write to you, dear children,**
because you know the Father.
I write to you, fathers,
because you know him who is from the beginning.
I write to you, young men,
because you are strong,
and the word of God lives in you,
and you have overcome the evil one.

On Not Loving the World

[15] Do not love the world or anything in the world. If anyone loves the world, love for the Father is not in them. [16] For everything in the world—the lust of the flesh, the lust of the eyes, and the pride of life—comes not from the Father but from the world. [17] The world and its desires pass away, but whoever does the will of God lives forever.

According to Genesis 3, Fear is always the result of Sin that pushes us away from the Father's presence and put us into a place of darkness, guiltiness.

There are Five (5) Curses after the fall:

1) <u>Curse on the serpent</u> V15: "Cursed are you above all livestock and all wild animals!
   You will crawl on your belly
   and you will eat dust
   all the days of your life.
   [15] And I will put enmity
   between you and the woman,
   and between your offspring and hers;

    he will crush your head,
and you will strike his heel."

2) <u>Curse on the Woman</u> V16: ¹⁶ To the woman he said,
"I will make your pains in childbearing very severe;
with painful labor you will give birth to children.
Your desire will be for your husband,
and he will rule over you."

3) <u>Curse on the Man</u> V19: actually the Lord GOD could not put a Curse on ADAM, His Perfection, made according to His own image, but instead He cursed the Ground, through the Man behavior or Sin, but That "silent curse or should I say unspoken Curse "on the man is found in the Bible in diverse places: (Romans 6:23; Ezekiel 33:13; Genesis2:17).

4) <u>Curse on the Body bringing Death</u>: see above references. So what kills the man is not the curse, rather the consequences of sin, brought by disobedience in his life.

5) <u>Curse on the Ground</u> V17: ¹⁷ To Adam he said, "Because you listened to your wife and ate fruit from the tree about which I commanded you, 'You must not eat from it,'

    "Cursed is the ground because of you;
through painful toil you will eat food from it
all the days of your life.
¹⁸ It will produce thorns and thistles for you,
and you will eat the plants of the field.

Notes: *The Curse that a man pronounces against another man, can be reverse, can be cancelled ; but the Curse that GOD himself pronounces upon creation, or man cannot be redeemed or cancelled by no one else; That's why Jesus could come and redeem us from the law of sin and Death. That says:* **"The soul that sinneth shall die".**

1 Peter 2:5-9

⁴ For if God did not spare angels when they sinned, but sent them to hell, putting them in chains of darkness to be held for judgment; ⁵ if he did not spare the ancient world when he brought the flood on its ungodly people, but protected Noah, a preacher of righteousness, and seven others; ⁶ if he condemned the cities of Sodom and Gomorrah by burning them to ashes, and made them an example of what is going to happen to the ungodly; ⁷ and if he rescued Lot, a righteous man, who was distressed by the depraved conduct of the lawless ⁸ (for that righteous man, living among them day after day, was tormented in his righteous soul by the lawless deeds he saw and heard)— ⁹ if this is so, then the Lord knows how to rescue the godly from trials and to hold the unrighteous for punishment on the day of judgment.

A) This is the **first plan of the Devil, Lucifer or Satan** that fall apart and did not succeed.
B) Now he (Satan) comes with another plan: meanwhile the first plan was the "coup d'état" in Heaven, becoming God himself, then stealing Adam's power and authority.
This time around, his plan was to pollute the seed, so that **CHRIST** will not come (refer to what the lord GOD promised in genesis 3:15).
He knew that, by stopping the coming of the One who will crash his head, he could keep that right of having the dominion stolen from Adam forever.
Being back in the second heaven with his fellow angels. He now plots to send them down on earth in the time of NOAH, when men began to multiply:

*"¹ When human beings began to increase in number on the earth and daughters were born to them, ² **the sons of God** saw that the daughters of humans were beautiful, and they married any of them they chose. ³ Then the LORD said, "My Spirit will not contend with humans forever, for they are mortal; their days will be a hundred and twenty years."*
⁴ The Nephilim were on the earth in those days—and also afterward—when the sons of God went to the daughters of humans and had children by them. They were the heroes of old, men of renown.
⁵ The LORD saw how great the wickedness of the human race had become on the earth, and that every inclination of the thoughts of the human heart was only evil all the time. ⁶ The LORD regretted that he had made human beings on the earth, and his heart was deeply troubled. ⁷ So the LORD said, "I will wipe from the face of the earth the human race I have created—and with them the animals, the birds and the creatures that move along the ground—for I regret that I have made them."

Here "sons of God, talks about the fallen angels of Lucifer's rebellion... Now I want you to understand the prophetic word: Many of the preachers of the Gospel thought that God destroyed Noah's world because of great sins! Uhmm...yes and no.... But moreover , because in the prophetic plan of YAHVEH, <u>the mixture of fallen angels seeds with the women (daughters of men) was the abomination that could have caused the almighty to see His plan destroyed, unfulfilled down on the road</u>; Reason why He decided to destroy that world by sending the Flood so that the Messiah still come to rescue mankind..

Here we come to the understanding of where are those fallen angels that sinned with daughters of men?? Well, read with me **Genesis 6:7** then jump to **2 Peter 3:4-5**.

The fallen angels' topic is very interesting that it will allow us to make the transition and start a new window of revelations:

The Five (5) Underworlds

Since then, those Fallen angels were sent by GOD himself to the underworld place, where they are chained till today, awaiting the last judgment into the lake of Fire.
Let's study and receive now the revelation of these worlds.

1) **Sheol or Hades:** A number of words in the original languages of the Bible have been translated by some English-language versions as *hell*. While there is definitely an end-time lake of fire for the wicked (e.g. Matthew 13:41-42, Revelation 19:20, 20:14), two of those original words, the Hebrew *Sheol* and the Greek *Hades*, merely mean *death*, or *the grave - the place where the dead sleep in peaceful unconsciousness* (e.g. Ecclesiastes 9:5) until their resurrection (see The Last Day).Isaiah 38:10; JOB 21:13.There is no period, no time gap between Death and hell, no purgatory place : Instantly to the presence of the Lord if you are born again, or instantly to hell if not born again (accepting Jesus as your savior and living your life according to GOD's laws).It's a place of Torments and fire remember the story of the rich man and Lazarus in Luke 16:23-24/27-28
2)

Biblical Scriptures:
- "But if The Lord creates something new, and the ground opens its mouth, and swallows them up, with all that belongs to them, and they go down alive into Sheol, then you shall know that these men have despised The Lord...So they and all that belonged to them went down alive into Sheol; and the earth closed over them, and they perished from the midst of the assembly." (Numbers 16:30, 33 RSV)
- "The Lord kills and brings to life; He brings down to Sheol and raises up." (1 Samuel 2:6 RSV)
- "like Sheol let us swallow them alive and whole, like those who go down to the pit" (Proverbs 1:12 RSV)
- "Shall I ransom them from the power of Sheol? Shall I redeem them from Death? O Death, where are your plagues? O Sheol, where is your destruction?" (Hosea 13:14 RSV)
- "What man can live and never see death? Who can deliver his soul from the power of Sheol?" (Psalms 89:48 RSV)
- "But you are brought down to Sheol, to the depths of the pit. (Isaiah 14:15 RSV)
- "Though they dig into Sheol, from there shall my hand take them; though they climb up to heaven, from there I will bring them down." (Amos 9:2 RSV)
- "And they do not lie with the fallen mighty men of old who went down to Sheol with their weapons of war, whose swords were laid under their heads, and whose shields are upon their bones; for the

terror of the mighty men was in the land of the living." (Ezekiel 32:27 RSV)

Hades
- "For thou wilt not abandon my soul to Hades, nor let thy Holy One see corruption." (Acts 2:27 RSV)
- "He foresaw and spoke of the resurrection of the Christ, that He was not abandoned to Hades, nor did His flesh see corruption." (Acts 2:31 RSV)
- "And the living one; I died, and behold I am alive for evermore, and I have the keys of Death and Hades." (Revelation 1:18 RSV)
- "And I saw, and behold, a pale horse, and its rider's name was Death, and Hades followed him; and they were given power over a fourth of the earth, to kill with sword and with famine and with pestilence and by wild beasts of the earth." (Revelation 6:8 RSV)
- "And the sea gave up the dead in it, Death and Hades gave up the dead in them, and all were judged by what they had done." (Revelation 20:13 RSV).

3) **Paradise:** From Adam all the way to Jesus, the paradise was on Earth, I should say: was part of the underworld places. After Jesus resurrection, He took the Paradise to Heaven, where mansions are built for the saints. Luke 16:19-31
Luke 23:43; Before Jesus went up to Heaven, He went down to Paradise, took the key of death, went to preach to the spirits in captivity then removed paradise from his initial place to Heaven. Glory to Jesus! Matthew 27:51-54 and Ephesians 4:7-10.

4) **PIT or Bottomless Pit or Pit of Hell:** Place of Demons, the spirits of the pre-adamic world tormenting the world of today, possessing human bodies. Luke 8:26-33; Mark 5:31.

   Thousands of millions of demons are released from the pit by human, when they offer sacrifices to the devil: by abortion, murder, magic ritual shading and the drinking of human blood, vampires, etc… Those acts call demons out from the Pit.
   They are different kind of demons according to the geographic place where the country is and what people offer as sacrifices to Satan; link to their tradition, cultures and human history. Revelation 9:1-11
   In our next Chapter we will talk more about these demons and their activities by month and culture. ***Stay tune!***

   As soon as the church is raptured and the tribulation starts, a star (Satan or Apollyon) falls down from heaven to the earth, receive the key (permission) to release those demons.

   Prophet note: Don't shake the hand of the Devil even when you are covered by the blood of Jesus, he will surely slap your mouth down.

   We are commanded not to go to the enemy's camp naked and think one second that GOD will protect us, if He did not send us. GOD is a GOD of Commands.

5) **Tartaros:** Place where the fallen angels who slept with the daughters of men in Genesis 6 are chained by GOD.

Jude 6-7; 2 Peter2:4-9. They left the second heaven, came down and slept with human daughters. The bible says that out of that union giants were born unto men… 1 Peter 3:18-19 .Tartaros on the other hand, lay as far beneath Hades (i.e. beneath the deepest recesses of the flat earth) as the sky lay above the earth.

The Lord Jesus went down to Tutorus to preach to those fallen angels and proclaim to them that HE made It, in spite of the tentative of invasion; HE came and did His job, therefore They are defeated. Hallelujah!

6) **Lake of Fire:** Matthew 25:41. This place is still empty from now, but will be filled by the devil, Satan and the false prophets and demons after the last judgment is pronounced by YAHVEH.

   Since the time of the resurrection of the Master till now, there are only Four (4) underworlds operating; but at the end of ages, all these underworlds will be put into the lake of fire forever and ever. Amen!

CLASSIFICATION OF DEMONS: BY MONTH

Matthew 12:43-45

Demons operate in the realm of the natural, on earth; they do not have bodies therefore they possess human being to execute their orders and achieve their will. Remember that they lost their bodies from the Pre-adamic world during the first Flood. Let's see some facts about them:

1) They can travel in space and time; from one place to another...they walk.
2) They know how to search or seek(They have intelligence) but no revelation
3) They get tired (seeking rest...Verse 43)
4) They are not all powerful
5) There are different levels of strength or hierarchy between demons
6) They can see and speak (mostly Lies)
7) They have their own will, personality and make their own decision
8) They have memory to remember, therefore they think
9) They can examine and analyze
10) They know how to plan
11) They work together; they are united;

Notes: Read these verses: Ephesians 4:27; Luke 10:19-20; Psalms 91:1
We got power in the mighty name of demons; it is written that in the name of Jesus, every knee shall bow, in heaven m on earth and under the earth. Amen!

After being cast out of heaven and then losing all his glory and position, Satan and his angels swore to defeat, or destroy man that GOD did created and gave him power, a greater position of worshipper. Demons are organized by legions and by order attacking human the best they could do daily. But here are the names of some demons I came across in the Bible and thought to share with you, classifying them by month.

- Belial   January
- Leviathan   February
- Satan   March
- Belphegor   April
- Lucifer   May
- Berith   June
- Beelzebub   July
- Astaroth   August
- Thammuz   September
- Baal   October
- Asmodai   November
- Molock or Moloch   December

So let's examine them, one by one now as they appear in the bible.

1) **BELIAL:** 2 Corinthians 6:14

   In Judaism, Belial is identified with Satan, the father of idolatrous nations under the name *Belhor*. He is the evilest being from who comes the 7 spirits of seduction that enter men at birth. Demon of January.

The source of impurity and lying, spirit of darkness. He will be opposed to the messiah, bound by The Lord and cast into the lake of fire forever.

He is the angel of lowliness, and ruler of this world...a seducer who claim to be the messiah. From Hebrew **Beli yo'il** meaning worthless or **Beli ol** meaning yokeless or never to rise **Beli ya'al**. Also from Babylonian godless: **Belili.**

He is the master in sin, Lie, arrogance, pride, Lust, fraud, injustice...Read: James 1:13-15; Exodus 32:1-7. He is the <u>**Calf Idol**</u> in the Desert with Israel.

Some scriptures:
Luke 8:26-33; Luke 9: 37-42; Matthew 13:25 (confusion – Seduction); 2 Timothy 3:1; 1Corinthians 5:7-8; 2 Corinthians 7:1; Galatians 5:19-21.

Belial is related to confusion and libertinage; idolatry and fornication: Numbers 25:1-5/13. He is a powerful king of Hell, created next after Lucifer. Studies report that he distributes senator ship, causes favor of friends and foes, gives excellent familiar spirits to people such as to medium, palm readers, etc.

As we have seen in the bible, with Israel when Moses is gone on the mountain on the Lord, Offerings and Sacrifices or gifts must be made to Belial or he will not answer the demands of the people.

Often times, is depicted with a man's body with talons instead of feet; and the head of a man with horns and ears of a bull and boar tusks: **Keeping the door of Hell.**

2) <u>**LEVIATHAN**</u>: From Hebrew **Liwjatan.**

Roughly meaning "Twisted" or "coiled". *He was a biblical multiheaded sea monster*: Psalms 74:13-14; JOB 41; Isaiah 27:1-2.
Now the Biblical Leviathan is considered to be a demon associated with Satan or the Devil and related to *Rahab or Dragon*: Isaiah 51:9.
In demonology, Leviathan is every aquatic demon. They are great liars and can also possess people...very difficult to deliver or cast out. They main targets are women specially. Demon of the month of February.

3) **SATAN-SATANA**: *Accuser or adversary.*

He plays many roles. He is the angel allowed by God to test mankind or evil rebellious demon .He is the enemy of GOD. Commonly known as *the Devil, Prince of Darkness, Beelzebub, Mephistopheles, Lucifer...*
Note that we have angelogy and demonology, two different categories of being and operations.
In Islam, Satan is called *Iblis*: chief of the angels until he disobeyed Allah by refusing to prostrate before Adam. Satan has evolved over many centuries in diverse forms and wicked ways. Demon of the month of March.
Let's see some of his attributes with scriptures:
- An enemy in war
- A Traitor in Battle: 1 Samuel 24:4; JOB 1:6-12
- An Accuser: Esther 3:7-11 (Haman & Mordecai) 1 Samuel 28:3-10; Revelation 12:10; 1 John 4:4; John 13:27; Isaiah 14;
  Ezekiel 28...
- Author of dispute and Confusion and war: Jude 9. Only the spirit of GOD convinces from Sin-Justice (Righteousness) and Judgment: John 16:8-11.

- Satan has no power of independence, action, but requires permission from GOD which he may not transgress: Zechariah 3:1-2; 1 Chronicles 21:1.
- Satan was able to provoke David the King to destroy Israel. 2 Samuel 24:1; 1 Samuel 16:14; 1Kings 22:
- An antagonist who puts obstacles in the way.
- Author of Division.

Below some of his credentials:

Among the Satanists, polytheists such as paganism, neopaganism (deity of other religions mixed together)
2kings 21:1-16 Manasseh's evil reign
Luke 10:18: Satan
Revelation 20:2: Old Serpent
Matthew 13:19: wicked one Matthew 6:13; John 5:19
John 10:10: Thief and robber
Act 20:29; Mathew 7:15: Wolf
He is the pretending spirit;
Matthew 4:3: The Tempter; Genesis 3:1-6
Revelation 13:1-18: The Beast
Revelation 17:3-17: the Antichrist
Revelation 12:9: The Dragon

4) **BELPHEGOR:**

In demonology, he is a demon who helps to make discoveries. How many of you know that all discoveries are not from GOD, but the devil?!
He seduces people by suggesting them ingenious inventions that will make them rich, celebs. His power is strong in April. He is depicted as a beautiful woman or a horrible naked and horned man, with claws instead of hands and, hairy beard: His name comes from the Semitic god Baal Peor. Demon of April.

5) **LUCIFER:** Isaiah 14:12; Luke 10:18

Lucifer is a Latin word of two (2): **Lux** (Light) and **Fero** (to bear or to bring). He is a Light-Bearer or Light-Bringer. He is the symbol of the deity of <u>VOODO</u> religion.
In the Bible, that name is linked to the signs of Zodiac: JOB 38:32 and the Aurora: Psalms 109:3 or the King of Babylon: Isaiah 14:12; Revelation 2:23; 2 Peter 1:19; Revelation 22:16. The name Lucifer and Satan, are just twin identical names, but the attribute or function of each as attribute in the action therein are totally different. Even though that name was given by GOD from the beginning, but to men he is well known as Satan, the accuser of the brethren. Notice the fifth word of the text—***Lucifer.*** It is not a proper name but the Latin word for 'morning star.' The word ***Lucifer*** occurs four times in the Vulgate: Isa 14:12, Job 11:17, Job 38:32, and 2 Peter 1:19. In Job 11:17, the KJV renders the Hebrew word בקר as 'morning'. Demon of May.

6) **BERITH:** *Judges 8:33* ; Leviticus 19:31 ; 1 Samuel 28:3/7-10

In Demonology, He is a great duke of Hell, powerful and terrible. He has 26 legions of demons under his command and he is the one who tells things of the past, present and future with true answers (The demon used by the entire mystic and magic and psychics world). He can also turn all metal into gold. He gives dignities to men and confirms or establishes them publicly .He speaks with a clear and subtly voice: He is a big Liar when not answering questions.

He is depicted as a soldier wearing red clothes. A golden crown and riding a red horse...he has red skin too.
His name comes from Baal-Berith: a form of Baal worshipped in Berith (Which city name became Beirut in Lebanon) .Some call **him Beal, Beale, Beall, Berithi, Bolfry or Bofry** (In Necromancy).Demon of June.

7) <u>**BEELZEBUB:**</u> Matthew 12:24; 2 Kings 1:16/V3

Beelzebub or Baal-zebub: Chief god in the Canaanite; the prince of demons; lord of the flies. In the Old Testament, the King Ahaziah fell ill; he sent messengers to call upon Baal-zebub: 2 Kings 1:2-3; Matthew 10:25; Mark 3:22; Luke 11:18-19.Demon of July.

He is placed among the five most powerful demons in Hell:
a) **Lucifer**
b) **Satan**
c) **Astaroth**
d) **Berith**
e) **Beelzebub.**
He is considered as the chief lieutenant of Lucifer, the emperor of hell and presides over ***<u>the Order of the Fly among the fallen angels.</u>*** He comes after Lucifer and Leviathan.

8) <u>**ASTAROTH:**</u> Judges 2:13

In demonology, he is a king of hell: Being Lucifer the emperor, and Satan a seducer of Women. He has three (3) main assistants' demons: **Aamon / Pruslas / Barbatos.**

He is depicted as a nude man with dragon-like wings, hands and feet: wearing a crown, holding a serpent in one hand and riding a wolf or dog. He is demon of first hierarchy who seduces by means of laziness and vanity.
He teaches mathematical sciences and handicrafts; he can make men invisible and lead them to hidden treasures. He answers any question formulated to him. This demon is of August.

9) **THAMMUZ:** Hebrews 11:35-37

In demonology, he is a demon of low hierarchy or category. He is the one that stimulates men to torture other people, and is in charge of fire guns, artillery. This demon is of September.

- **THE PRINCE OF DARKNESS**: *The DEVIL*

He is the central embodiment of evil, having variety of names: Satan, Lucifer, Mephistopheles, and Beelzebub...
Devil in Greek diabolos meaning to slander or Deva= angel in Indo-European language. Zechariah 3:1; 1 Peter 5:8; Luke 10:18; Numbers 22:22.
He has a nick name: prince of this world: John 12:31; John 14:30; Revelation 12:9; Genesis 3:1-7; JOB 1:9; JOB 2:4; Matthew 13:39; John 8:44.
In the game Dungeons & Dragons devils are known as **Boatezu** or **Tamar'ri.**
Also some actual symbols used by witches and magicians for summoning & protection.

10) **BAAL:** or Baalim Plural

   Baal, son of EL was chief god in Ugarit, inherited by Canaanites.
   The Syrian name of Baal as storm and Thunder Mountain-god was *Hadad*; or *Baal-Hadad*: The lord of storm, governing rain and germination of plants.
   On the other hand, **MOT** was the god of death and **Yamm**, the god of the sea or Leviathan: 1 Chronicles 12:5. This demon has his power manifest mostly in October.

11) **ASMODAI:** Persian god. Manifest his power in the month of November.

   He is the chief of all demons, under the direct command of **Angra Mainyu**: The principal of evils. He fills the hearts of men with anger and vengeful desires. He pushes men to abandon good and do evil instead. He is also in charge of Night- wedding (happening in dreams) and kills the man or woman involved each time that person gets married to someone else. We have seen this happening a lot, especially from our traditions and cultures, all over the world; Impeding the consummation of sexual act: He is the protector of Homosexuals and lesbians. He uses homosexuality to seduce, also by possessing them and leading them to Gambling.

   He has 72 legions of demons under his command. The way he's depicted is with chest of a man, goat legs ending with talons, serpent tail, and three (3) heads and riding a lion with dragon's wings and Neck. Leviticus 20:1-2.

12) **MOLOCK / MOLOCH:**

This name gave also *Milcom* or *Molech* which gave birth to "*Malcolm X*". 1 Kings 11:5; Jeremiah 7:31; Jeremiah 19:5. This is a powerful demon December.

His status or *altar* had a construction similar to a dome (on which the body was surmounted) with fire always lit. He is the demon responsible of Human sacrifices, especially infants and children during war, strikes, whatever event bringing death of children for purpose of power, position or victory in the spiritual dark world.

Moloch comes from the Semitic word *Melek* or *Melekh* the King, He makes mothers weep by stealing and killing their children and passing them through the fire to be sacrificed. He was also the god of the Ammonites in Babylon and of the Moabites.

Salomon, the King built an altar to Molock and Manasseh sacrificed his son through fire on one of those altars in 2 Kings 21: 3-6.

The demon **Chemosh** was the abomination of the Moabites in 1 Kings 11:7

WHY GOD so *SERIOUS* with you?

Strike your Enemy 100% to Death.

I would like to start this great revelation by telling you that everything here in this book follows a pattern, which is **the march of biblical prophecy** and what the Lord our GOD did and why he did it...In other words, here you will understand GOD's plan perfectly. By the end of this prophetic journey, you will know without a shadow of doubt, what is the depth, the High, the width, the Length of GOD's wisdom and knowledge and how much **HE** can just do with us, little Jacob.

When Israel invaded the Promised Land, GOD told them not to leave any of the enemy alive. This may shock some of you, but you are about to come across the **<u>GOD</u>** with whom you can't resist nor fight against. He knows what he is doing! Do you know that GOD sees the future for the present and the present in the future?

It is recorded in the bible that Joshua spared giants in three (3) different cities while GOD commanded him not. He disobeyed the orders. Those cities are:

Gaza - Ashdod - Gath. Joshua 11:21-22. By doing such think, I should say by having that <u>*lackadaisical attitude*</u>, Joshua was about to be one of the pillar of GOD's plan failure without knowing it. Guess what! **GOD did not let this happen**.

Later on, the story goes on and the bible relates that:

1. Samson, one of the mighty men in Israel at his time got in trouble in **Gaza** (Judges 16).
2. The Ark of covenant of GOD's glory was stolen and lost in **Ashdod** (1 Samuel 5 and 6).
3. And that Goliath challenged and immobilized the army and troops of Israel for 40 days in **Gath** (1 Samuel 17). You think these are coincidence events? Absolutely not. These events would have not happened *if* Joshua *did obey* GOD and smite the enemy 100% as commanded.

Let me bring you to another event here in 2 Kings 13:14-19 (Please read it).
The king-the window-the Bow and arrows. The prophet asked the king to shoot eastward for a prophetic reason. But see what was done!

"A simple instruction from GOD requires our total Obedience from us. If you magnify, GOD will manifest."
Listen! GOD is so serious when a prophetic seed is involved in his Plan, in His Purpose, in His design and in His objective.

It always happen when GOD has declared, called or chosen something in His divine Plan, that will shake the world and fulfill *His WILL* in the future.

4. 1 Samuel 15:1-9

Now let's see and read this passage to understand and find out what the Almighty GOD said to Israel when they came out of Egypt (Slavery).

V-1-9 reads: *"Samuel also said unto Saul, The Lord sent me to anoint thee to be King over his people, over Israel: now therefore hearken thou unto the voice of the words of the Lord.*
*Thus saith the Lord of Hosts, I remember that which **Amalek** did to Israel, how he laid wait for him in the way, when he came up from Egypt. Now go and smite **Amalek**, and utterly destroy all that they have, and spare them not; but slay man and woman, infant, and suckling, ox and sheep, camel and ass..." Verse 9"But Saul and the people spared **Agag** and the best of the sheep and..."*

Wait a minute, I want you to understand here what's going on and for that, allow me to bring you back to the beginning of the **cause**, to allow you to grasp the **effect** thereafter. Genesis 36:10-12 (Amalek Origin).

You can see that Amalek did evil, trying **to oppose GOD's plan** again for future redemption; used by Satan; He tried to eradicate the entire nation of Israel.

Uhmm! Does this seem familiar to you today, talking about Iran?

Consequence: **No Jesus coming, no Salvation, and Lost forever!**
If I was given the liberty to speak like "a street fighter" I would say: "That Pissed GOD off" **ooops!**

Same thing happen with Moses here in Exodus 17:8-16.

Then again in Numbers 24:15-20 and as you read, you will find out that V19-20 equal 1 Samuel 30:17...Finally back here; It happened with Saul, the king.

Saul, the King disobeyed GOD order by sparing Agag, king of Amalekites.

Listen! Cheaters never WIN, and winners never cheat. Sometime, *we don't just see the consequences of our actions*, but believe me now: if <u>not on us</u>, it will be upon the next generation <u>*or someone else always pays the price*</u> of our disobedience. 1 Samuel 15:22-23 / V28-29

Ok, let's see what happen when we don't do what the Holy Spirit or the prophet of GOD commands us to do. **1 Samuel 30:1-2 and Verse 4-8 and Verse 17-19.**

Now, for many years I asked the Lord why Saul the King was rejected just for sparing Agag and taking food for his people; while the king David killed took the woman of Uriah his general and made her his wife... *Why David was not rejected*??? A one Million question!

We see the prophet Samuel's call to find a replacement for disobedient King Saul. The Lord directs Samuel to a shepherd boy named David, whom he anoints as the future King. David is called to serve as a musician in Saul's court. He dramatically slays the giant warrior, Goliath.

Here the prophetic answers:
1) David repented and wrote psalms 51;
2) David consulted the Lord GOD prior engaging in battle and after receiving the Order from GOD; He pursued the Amalekites and utterly destroyed the entire Amalek's descendants. [7] Then David said to Abiathar the priest, the son of Ahimelek, "Bring me the ephod." Abiathar brought it to him,

⁸ and David inquired of the LORD, "Shall I pursue this raiding party? Will I overtake them?"

3) "Pursue them," he answered. "You will certainly overtake them and succeed in the rescue."
4) He understood that a prophetic Seed was involved and that if not today, never will he Rise again.
5) Obedience is better than Sacrifice, David knew that very well.
6) By doing so, He preserved GOD's plan of redemption through Christ Jesus and GOD was so pleased that He called Him, ***"Man after my Own Heart"***.

7) ***The sin of David, involved himself (1 Corinthians 6: 15-20), his flesh and not the entire nation, therefore, after he repented, GOD is merciful to forgive. But Saul's sin, involved the entire nation of Israel and the coming Messiah, the seed of the woman. It was a sin against GOD's plans directly, therefore, no repentance accepted, and no tolerance at all. The entire destiny of GOD's children was jeopardized by one man. GOD Got so Serious About IT!*** Like one's would said: This was a matter of National security!

Note:
Be careful when you involve GOD's kingdom, GOD's people, and GOD's name by your sins or wrong doing. GOD is not mocked...! When it comes to GOD's children Destiny, GOD will always raise a standard against the enemy.

- ❖ In The year the King Uzziah die, Isaiah received a new revelation from God
- ❖ When Moses dies, Joshua entered into the fullness of his ministry. His season started.
- ❖ When Saul was rejected by GOD, the prophet Samuel was directed to stop grieving and weeping, to go and anoint a new King and move on to the next step of GOD's agenda. Exodus 23:20-31

WHAT REALLY HAPPEN WHEN JESUS DIE?

Well, I will start this chapter full of amazing revelations by asking these questions to you: Are you *dead* or *Alive*? Are you *IN* or *OUT*?

JOHN 19:40-42

"**Then** took they the body of Jesus, and wound it in linen clothes with the spices, as the manner of the Jews is to bury.

Now in the place where he was crucified there was a garden; and in the garden a new sepulcher, wherein was never man yet laid. There laid they Jesus therefore because of the Jews' preparation day; for the sepulcher was nigh at hand."

The bible says this*: "But as it is written, Eye hath not seen, nor ear heard, neither have entered into the heart of man, the things which GOD hath prepared for them that love him."* 1 Corinthians 2:9

What I am about to reveal to you today is in my opinion the most wonderful revelation of the Cross so far. What really happen at the cross of Calvary when Jesus die?

We know by now that the LORD Jesus die on Friday and the same day was put in the Tomb. As prophesied, HE will rise on the third day, which is Sunday: The First day of the Hebrew calendar Week.

The bible says that Jesus is the First fruit of the creation; Remember talking about fruit is always related to a field, a Vineyard or in this case, A Garden. Leviticus 23:9-11.

As we read John 20:1 we see that there was a stone placed in front of the Tomb, sealed. The stone here symbolize the Law that kills, the mind and way of thinking of men that bring death .Death could not hold him back for these reasons that the Holy Spirit revealed to his servant:

1) To fulfill God's prophecy: *Three days after, He will resurrect from the dead*.
2) To reveal to the world that He is the First fruit of the creation indeed that giveth Life and life abundantly.
3) To reveal to us that He is the DOOR
4) That He is the second Adam that overcame sin and Death and came out Victorious. While the First Adam failed drastically. Before I even go deeper into this, allow me to ask you these simple questions that will bring about revelation into your spiritual being: What was the Sin that the first Adam and Eve committed? **_Eating of the Fruit_**.
Now, again, where did Satan stole the power and Glory That GOD gave to Adam? **_In The Garden of Eden._** Genesis 3:1-7

The first Adam and Eve , by eating the fruit of Disobedience, of the tree failed into sin and Death, But The Second Adam ***Jesus , being the first fruit of GOD , by eating his body and partaking in his sufferings and death , we are saved, redeemed, delivered …Death Has no more power. His resurrection that Sunday Morning was not only to be the first fruit, but furthermore, to fulfill and finish what the plan of GOD; Linking both prophetic events in one day.***
It was GOD's way of saying to Satan, what started in the Garden had to end in the Garden; This was a Rematch between GOD and Lucifer.
If you read carefully the two scriptures of John 19:40-42 and Genesis 2:8-10 you will see exactly the same environment on both sides… GOD did it to fulfill his marvelous plan. Jesus

Christ Lived and step by step was accomplishing which was declared by GOD in the Old Testament.

In Chapter 18 and verse 1-2 of John, we see that Jesus (as often) went to Gethsemane's Garden to Pray and rest; by the way Gethsemane means **_"Place of Oil Pressed"._** But what I want to point out here is verse 2 that says:" And Judas also, which betrayed him, _**knew the place**_: for Jesus often times resorted thither with his disciples." **Never allow your enemies to discover your secret place lest they destroy you.** Do you know that the night Our Lord was arrested, Peter who followed him far away by distance, was standing at the door waiting, while the Master being falsely accused by Caiaphas the High Priest and the Sanhedrin.

2011-2014: SEASON OF GOD'S EAGLES

PART I: *The Law of Becoming*

Introduction

In this lesson we will be talking about eagles. I have reserved this subject for last for two reasons. More is said about eagles in Scripture than any other one bird. The other reason—maybe more important—the eagle is my favorite bird as far as scriptural bird watching is concerned, and the Lord has used the truth taught in the Word of God concerning the eagle in my own life personally a number of times over. For that reason, it is a precious study to me.

The Lord gave me one verse concerning the eagle that we will be thinking about upon which I am still resting. These all have a special significance to me, and I think that I can share some of the blessings with you from them. *In this season of end times, the Lord GOD is calling for his children, servants, sons and daughters , for the church to step into the <u>Eagle season</u> of their Lifetime.* **NOW!**

I have mentioned to you before that the eagle is mentioned some twenty-six times in the Scripture by way of illustration. We are not counting the times that the eagle is simply mentioned as a fowl, but by way of the eagle used for illustration, it is something like twenty-six times.

Perhaps the reason for that is the amazement of Solomon concerning the eagle. Solomon was the wisest man who ever lived, and he certainly had a special gift of wisdom from God, as you know from your study of the Word of God. He said that he was mystified by some things, and he named them in chapter 30 of the book of Proverbs, verse 18.

He said:

Proverbs 30

18 *There be three things which are too wonderful for me, yea, four which I know not:*

He said, "There are three things that simply amaze me, actually four. I don't have the explanation for all that I see in connection with them, but they amaze me." Then verse 19:

Proverbs 30

19 *The way of an eagle in the air; the way of a serpent upon a rock; the way of a ship in the midst of the sea; and the way of a man with a maid.*

He said, "All of these things are so intrinsically interesting that it is difficult to explain all of the activities related to them." We notice, particularly, the first statement of verse 19. He said, "Something that is too wonderful for me, something that I never get tired of watching, and something that I can't fully explain is the way of an eagle in the air."

Eagles Used as Illustrations

I am going to suggest to you the various things about the eagle which are used as illustrations, and I am going to give you the Scripture references. If you are interested, you can pursue them at your own leisure because we are only going to talk about four of them. The bird watchers in the Bible observing the eagle were impressed with the strength of her wings and used them as an illustration for redemption in Exodus, chapter 19, verse 4, and in Revelation, chapter 12, verse 14.

They were impressed, likewise, with the swiftness of the flight of the eagle and used it as an illustration of the swift judgment of God upon those who were disobedient in Deuteronomy, chapter 28, verse 29; Jeremiah, chapter 48, verse 40; Jeremiah, chapter 49, verse 22; Isaiah, chapter 8, verse 1; Jeremiah, chapter 4, verse 13; and Habakkuk, chapter 1, verse 8. All of these are references to the swiftness of judgment.

As the eagle flies swiftly to their prey, so does the judgment of God come. Each one of these verses has a little different flavor to it, so it isn't empty repetition.

The swiftness of the eagle is also used as an illustration of the brevity of life. We had already established Job as a bird watcher; and in Job, chapter 9, verse 26, when he observed the eagle in her swift flight, he was reminded of how swiftly the days of our lives pass by. Interestingly enough, Solomon wrote of the swiftness of the eagle, and it has always been amusingly interesting to me the swiftness of the eagle as it is illustrated in how quickly your money gets away from you. I suspect that all of us have had some problem along that line. You have money and then the first thing you know, you don't have it.

When the biographies of both Saul and Jonathan were being written in II Samuel, chapter 1, verse 23, the swiftness of the eagle was used as an illustration of their prowess as warriors. In Ezekiel, chapter 17, verses 3 and 7, the swiftness of the eagle was used to illustrate the mighty power and the swift judgment that the king of Babylon brought upon those who were disobedient to his rule and to his reign.

You have heard of the bald eagle. The bald eagle is called a *bald eagle* not because he has no feathers on his head, as men have no hair on their head when they are bald, but because the feathers on the eagle's head are white; and at a distance, it gives the appearance of baldness—hence the name, *bald eagle*. The baldness of the eagle was used by Micah in chapter 1, verse 16, to describe the devastating judgment that God was going to bring on disobedient people. Micah said, "Your baldness will increase as the baldness of the eagle."

There are several references to nesting habits of the eagle. The fact that the eagle builds her nest on the highest crag and in the topmost part of the tree in each instance is used as an illustration of the foolishness of pride. In Job, chapter 39, verses 27-30, Job's pride was rebuked by a reference to the nesting habits of the eagle.

In Jeremiah, chapter 49, verse 16, Jeremiah said, "Though Israel raised herself to the pinnacle as high as the eagle's nest, even to the starry sky, God would bring her down to her own level." In Obadiah, verse 4, the same truth is emphasized concerning Moab: "Though she builds her nest as high as the eagle's nest, there certainly would be a coming down."

In Psalm 103, verse 5, a habit connected with the eagle's molting process describes the rejuvenation that is possible for all who place their faith and their trust in God, and then the unusual strength of the eagle as far as her ability to last in long flights is concerned, is used by Isaiah to illustrate the enduring strength that is made possible for all believers in Isaiah, chapter 40, verse 31.

Then the eagle is used in several prophetic visions such as Ezekiel, chapter 1, verse 10, Ezekiel, chapter 10, verse 14, and Revelation, chapter 4, verse 7. There the eagle is used to describe one of the four descriptions of the living creatures, known as the *cherubim* and the *seraphim*. In Daniel, chapter 2, verse 4, the nation of Babylon is described as having great strength by picturing her as an animal that had eagle's wings.

I think you will find a perusal of these Scriptures at your own convenience profitable to you, and it is very possible that the Lord will give you some thoughts about them that I haven't even made an attempt to suggest.

An Illustration of Deliverance and Redemption

I would like for us to look at four of the passages that I gave you for the spiritual lessons and illustrations that we can draw from them. I would like to begin by saying that the first spiritual lesson that we may learn from the habits of the eagle is an illustration of deliverance and redemption. Turn back, please, to the book of Exodus, chapter 19. You will notice the address of Moses to the children of Israel after they had come out of the land of Egypt after they had been delivered from the hand of the Egyptians. I think it would be a good idea for us to just begin with the first verse. Notice as we read together:

Exodus 19

1	*In the third month, when the children of Israel were gone forth out of the land of Egypt, the same day came they into the wilderness of Sinai.*
2	*For they were departed from Rephidim, and were come to the desert of Sinai, and had pitched in the wilderness; and there Israel camped before the mount.*
3	*And Moses went up unto God, and the LORD called unto him out of the mountain, saying, Thus shalt thou say to the house of Jacob, and tell the children of Israel;*
4	*Ye have seen what I did unto the Egyptians, and how I bare you on eagles' wings, and brought you unto myself.*

Actually, if you read the account of the exodus of the children of Israel from the land of Egypt, you know that they walked; but if you keep in mind that behind them was the Egyptian army and before them was a body of water which they could not cross in their own strength, you will realize that their deliverance was divine. As Moses thought upon the divine deliverance—without the aid of human effort—there came to his mind a picture he had often seen of a mother eagle putting her eaglets on her wings and flying great distances with them. They did absolutely nothing but rest upon the wings of the mother. They were carried about through no strength of their own. It was all upon the mother eagle.

When we think of salvation by grace without the aid of human effort, I don't think we can find a better illustration than this one of the eagle. Just picture in your mind's eye how those little eaglets are supported entirely by the one who bears them on her wings. Can you imagine any of those little eagles claiming any credit for the journey, even being able to say, "I at least had to get on the wings." Yet, I know any number of people who are so afraid to say that salvation is by grace alone—without the aid of human effort.

They say, "Well, you have got to at least believe," and they want to take some merit even for the faith that they put in the Lord Jesus Christ. Yet, we are told in Ephesians, chapter 2, that even the faith with which we believe is a gift of God. We can't even claim any credit for that. The wonderful thing about it is the eagle's wings are always underneath as long as we need them, but there will be times when we must do without them, as we shall see.

Comparable to this verse in the book of Exodus is one in the very last book of the Bible, the book of Revelation, chapter 12. While you are turning to Revelation, chapter 12, let me remind you that this chapter is the record of a sign. The book of Revelation is full of signs. People are concerned about the signs in the book of Revelation, and they wonder how anybody could know what the signs mean. Let me suggest here that any signs, any symbols in the book of Revelation that need an explanation is explained either in the book of Revelation or somewhere else in the Word of God.

Notice what I said—any sign which needs an explanation. There are some signs and some symbols that don't need an explanation. If the explanation is needed, the explanation is found either in the book of Revelation or somewhere else in the Word of God. Will you notice verse 1:

Revelation 12

1   *And there appeared a great wonder in heaven; a woman clothed with the sun, and the moon under her feet, and upon her head a crown of twelve stars:*

We do not have time for a detailed study of the book of Revelation, so you are just going to have to accept by faith what I say if this is new material to you, but this woman is the nation of Israel. Then in verse 2:

Revelation 12

2   *And she being with child cried, travailing in birth, and pained to be delivered.*

3	And there appeared another wonder in heaven; and behold a great red dragon [the dragon is the devil], having seven heads and ten horns, and seven crowns upon his heads.
4	And his tail drew the third part of the stars of heaven, and did cast them to the earth: and the dragon stood before the woman which was ready to be delivered, for to devour her child as soon as it was born.
5	And she brought forth a man child [the man child is the Lord Jesus Christ], who was to rule all nations with a rod of iron: and her child was caught up unto God, and to his throne.

The child was the Lord Jesus Christ. After the Lord Jesus Christ was born and fulfilled His purpose on the earth, He ascended up into Heaven in the last part of verse 5. Notice verse 6:

Revelation 12

6	And the woman fled into the wilderness, where she hath a place prepared of God that they should feed her there a thousand two hundred and threescore days.

Between verses 5 and verse 6 is the age of grace in which we live. In verse 6, the Tribulation has begun and this woman has to flee into the wilderness because of the persecution that was leveled against her. In verses 7-11, there is the story of the final rejection of Satan from Heaven. In verse 12, the middle of the Tribulation has occurred and judgment on the earth is going to increase, so you read in verse 12:

Revelation 12

12	Therefore rejoice ye heavens, and ye that dwell in them. Woe to the inhabiters of the earth and of the sea! for the devil is come down unto you, having great wrath, because he knoweth that he hath but a short time.

13	*And when the dragon saw that he was cast unto the earth, he persecuted the woman which brought forth the man child.*

The persecution of Israel increases in the tribulation period. What kind of trouble was Israel in in the land of Egypt? Persecution. That is the reason that she cried unto God, and God delivered her from the hand of Pharaoh. At the end of the age, yet future as we are concerned, during the Tribulation period, the nation of Israel is going to be in need of deliverance.

How is God going to provide that deliverance? In the same way that He provided it when He delivered her from Egypt. Look at verse 14:

Revelation 12

14	*And to the woman were given two wings of a great eagle, that she might fly into the wilderness, into her place, where she is nourished for a time, and times, and half a time* [three and one half years] *, from the face of the serpent.*
15	*And the serpent cast out of his mouth water as a flood after the woman, that he might cause her to be carried away of the flood.*
16	*And the earth helped the woman, and the earth opened her mouth, and swallowed up the flood which the dragon cast out of his mouth.*

At the beginning of Israel's history, redemption was the theme provided by an eagle. In the end of Israel's history, redemption is the theme illustrated by the strength of an eagle. We are borne—what was true of Israel in many ways—on eagles' wings. Salvation is by grace without the aid of human efforts.

An Illustration of Renewal

Turn to Psalm 103 and notice a molting habit of the eagle which the Spirit of God is pleased to use as an illustration of the rejuvenation that we as believers need from time to time. Let's begin reading with verse 1:

Psalm 103

1   *Bless the LORD, O my soul: and all that is within me, bless his holy name.*

2   *Bless the LORD, O my soul, and forget not all his benefits:*

3   *Who forgiveth all thine iniquities; who healeth all thy diseases;*

4   *Who redeemeth thy life from destruction; who crowneth thee with lovingkindness and tender mercies;*

5   *Who satisfieth thy mouth with good things;* [now notice] *so that thy youth is renewed like the eagle's.*

I wonder why David said this. He was familiar with the habits of eagles. Periodically, after a certain number of years, an eagle will go off to some distant point by itself. It will shed all of its old feathers and grow new feathers. It takes a period of time. Its claws will grow until new claws have appeared, the old claws being dead. When it leaves this secret place, it returns to its natural habitat looking like a young eagle, though it is many years old. This was the habit with which David was familiar when he said, "You know, God treats us like that. He meets our needs in such a fashion that our youth is renewed; our youth is restored to us just like the youth of an eagle."

I would like for you to notice that word *renew* there, because it is very significant to me that it is one of two Hebrew words which could have been used. The Spirit of God was pleased to use the Hebrew word *zered*, which may be translated by the word *rebuild* or by the word *repair*. It is interesting that when the Spirit of God said, "We may renew the strength of our youth like the eagles," that He used the very word that describes the process that I have shared with you.

Sometimes airplanes have to be put into the garage for repairs. Oftentimes the plane has so many hours on her. She is in the garage for repairs." It doesn't mean that she is broken down; it means that after so many flying hours, it has to be gone over completely. It needs to be renewed.

I hope that you are getting the lesson without a great deal of comment from me because surely you recognize that you and I need the same kind of renewal. You and I need to have the opportunity of renewing our experiences in the Lord, renewing our lives, so to speak.

For an illustration of what I am talking about, turn to the Ephesian letter, chapter 4. In this chapter of the Ephesian letter, we are told that we have been in right relationship to Jesus Christ through the new birth, and since we have that experience, there comes a time in our lives when we have to shed our feathers, when we have to get rid of the old claws. Those words are not actually used, but if you look at verse 22, you see:

Ephesians 4

22	*That ye put off concerning the former conversation the old man, which is corrupt according to the deceitful lusts;*
23	*And be renewed in the spirit of your mind;*
24	*And that ye put on the new man, which after God is created in righteousness and true holiness.*
25	*Wherefore putting away lying, speak every man truth with his neighbour: for we are members one of another.*

Sometimes when we gather together in a place like this, away from all of the ordinary demands of life, it provides an opportunity for us to have our youth renewed. Sometimes that is true physically if you do not play too hard, but if you have your spirit renewed, you go back home with a new vigor and a new strength you did not have, and you feel young spiritually again.

I just ask this question to provoke our thinking, but I wonder, haven't you felt sometimes that your relationship to the Lord is a dry and a dusty thing, sort of an old hat? You are really not enjoying it. You are going through the motions, but they really don't mean to you what they once did. Maybe what you need to do is to follow the practice of the eagle:

Get away somewhere and shed the old feathers and the old claws and sharpen the new ones, and be ready for new and interesting experiences.

An Illustration of God's Training

Turn to Deuteronomy, chapter 32, as Moses calls to our attention another practice of the eagle which is an illustration of God's training for us as His children. Notice the paragraph that begins with verse 11:

Deuteronomy 32

11	*As an eagle stirreth up her nest, fluttereth over her young, spreadeth abroad her wings, taketh them, beareth them on her wings:*
12	*So the LORD alone did lead him, and there was no strange god with him.*
13	*He made him ride on the high places of the earth, that he might eat the increase of the fields; and he made him to suck honey out of the rock, and oil out of the flinty rock;*
14	*Butter of kine, and milk of sheep, with fat of lambs, and rams of the breed of Bashan, and goats, with the fat of kidneys of wheat; and thou didst drink the pure blood of the grape.*

As Moses was thinking about God's provision for His people, he said, "God's people don't want God's best for them. They have to be trained to trust." Do you realize that? Trusting does not come easily. You have to be trained to trust, and Moses called to mind something that he had often seen high up on the mountain crag.

A mother eagle had been feeding the young eaglets for a long time, and as he observed their practices, he discovered that the mother eagle was frantically flapping her wings over the nest and, of all things, was pushing the eaglets out of the nest. There they were, plummeting down from that high mountain crag. Moses thought, like any of us would think, what a horrible thing that was to do, but before those little eaglets had fallen very far, the mother eagle had swooped down underneath them and caught them on her wings and was bearing them back up to the nest again.

This practice was repeated over and over again, and he saw the eaglets flying before it was over; but he also noticed something else, and that was that they always returned to the nest. The mother eagle could push them out of the nest, and it wasn't necessary any more for her to catch them. They could fly about by themselves, but they always returned to the nest.

Moses recorded something else that he had observed. Notice verses 11-12 again:

God Sometimes Stirs Up Our Nest

Deuteronomy 32

11	*As an eagle stirreth up her nest, fluttereth over her young, spreadeth abroad her wings, taketh them, beareth them on her wings:*
12	*So the LORD alone did lead him, and there was no strange god with him.*

The eagle finally tore up the nest. There is a tremendous lesson there. I just want to ask you, "Have you had your nest torn up?" Maybe you have been secure in what you were doing. You have been secure in your home or your work or whatever you are doing. Your plans have all been made. Things are going exactly like you want them and things couldn't be better, then your nest has been torn up, and you have wondered why. You have even complained about it. You have even objected to it, but you really don't need to because as the eagle had to tear up her nest to train her young to trust their God-given ability to fly, so God sometimes has to stir up our nest to teach us to trust Him.

Did you notice in verse 13: "He made him ride on the high places of the earth." If that nest had never been broken, those eagles would have stayed on that mountain crag, fed by their mother, never having had the thrill of flying on their own and soaring to the highest heights to see what it was to really trust God.

I am wondering if you realize that God may have to stir up your nest to accomplish His purpose in your life

Deuteronomy 32

11 *As an eagle stirreth up her nest, fluttereth over her young, spreadeth abroad her wings, taketh them, beareth them on her wings:*

12 *So the LORD alone did lead him, and there was no strange god with him.*

When God breaks up the nest, you do not have any problems. There are no strange gods; there is no false leadership.

We don't know what is going to happen. We may never be together again like we are now. The Lord may be here before there is time for another conference. He may not; I don't know; but will you try to remember that if for some reason God breaks up your nest, He has a purpose for it, and you will be the better for the experience whether you can believe it now or not.

Waiting On the Lord

One last thought: Isaiah, chapter 40, verse 31, is the verse that the Lord gave me in 1971. I have mentioned to some of you who have been with us here and in other meetings, that I have followed the practice for a number of years of asking God to give me a year verse. He directs my attention to some passage of Scripture for the year. As I have said, they are never calendar years; they don't always begin and end with January; sometimes they last longer than twelve months.

The verse that God gave me in 1989 has continued in my thinking up to this very moment. When I ask God to give me a verse that I can rest upon in the Word of God, I ask Him to give it to me in view of what He knows is going to come up in my life, something that I can rest upon. I may not need the verse at the time that He gives it to me, and I always know why He gave it to me before it is over with.

Some people say, "Well, how does He give it to you?" I don't close my Bible and drop it on the floor, then wherever it opens that is the verse that God gave me. I just study the Word and ask Him to direct my attention to a particular passage, and He always has. In 1989, He directed my attention to Isaiah, chapter 40, verse 31:

Isaiah 40

31 *But they that wait upon the LORD shall renew their strength; they shall mount up with wings as eagles; they shall run, and not be weary; and they shall walk, and not faint.*

Did you notice the word *renew* here? We had that word *renew* in Psalm 103, but this is an entirely new Hebrew word. This is the Hebrew word *chalaph*. The Hebrew word *kered* meant "to build and repair." This word *chalaph* describes a growing up or a sprouting up of a new plant. As a matter of fact, Job, in chapter 14 of his book, uses the word in just that way. You might turn back there to get the full significance of what this kind of renewal means. You see, there is more than one kind of renewal, and this kind of renewal is described in Job, chapter 14, the paragraph which begins with verse 7. Notice:

Job 14

7 *For there is hope of a tree, if it be cut down, that it will sprout* [there is the word chalaph] *again, and that the tender branch thereof will not cease.*

8 *Though the root thereof wax old in the earth, and the stock thereof die in the ground;*

9 *Yet through the scent of water it will bud, and bring forth boughs like a plant.*

You see, there was a time during this experience when the root waxed old in the ground, when there was apparently not any life in me left. Yet, as I waited upon the Lord, I found myself springing up like a tender plant out of the dry ground.

Something else I want to mention to you about this verse. Did you notice the order in which it is written? Notice:

Isaiah 40

31   ***But they that wait upon the LORD shall renew their strength; they shall mount up with wings as eagles; they shall run, and not be weary; and they shall walk, and not faint.***

It is backward, isn't it? Our order of progression is to walk, run, then to fly, but God put it backward to emphasize the power of His strength. You see, it is easy to fly. It is exhilarating to fly. You don't get bored flying, and there is a certain thrill to running because it is fast movement and things are happening.

But finally you get down to the walking stage, and here the Hebrew word for *walk* is a word that describes a man who is walking very slowly because of an exceedingly heavy weight upon his back. You can see what God says: If you wait upon the Lord, when you get to the walking stage where you have that heavy weight and you are plodding along and you don't know if you can take one more step forward, He is giving you a promise: "Thou shalt not faint."

PART II: *Eagle Vision and the Eagle anointing*

Here I would like to discuss about what the Lord revealed to me in the beginning of this end time season: The Supernatural ability to see with your spiritual eyes, things that the Most High GOD is doing now!

Here I would like to discuss about what the Lord revealed to me in the beginning of this end time season: The Supernatural ability to see with your spiritual eyes, things that the Most High GOD is doing now!

The Limitations of Sight

I heard a man once say "sight is a function of the eye; vision is a function of the heart". It's the capacity of your physical eyes to see what is tangible. It's the responsibility of those same eyes to perceive visible things. But the thing with these same eyes is that they are limited, bound and constricted to what already is, the present. They don't have the ability to see the invisible nor the capability of seeing the future or what maybe

Let's be real and look in the Church, The Body of Christ. At this moment through what can be seen, it is apparent that The Church is weak, broke, afraid and divided. The Bride of Christ has acne and pimples all over the body. She has more wrinkles than a 90 year old. The big giant of Jesus' body has been chained down to the earth's surface, held down and made captive by midgets and dwarfs of the kingdom of darkness. The church is not a voice in society, but a mere echo. The world has simply left the Christians to get on with their 'religion'. To the world, the Christians are a joke. David said in Psalms 42:3 "My tears have been my food day and night, while they continually say to me, "Where is your God?" The world is saying the same thing 'Where is your God? Where's this Jesus whom you say is so great and powerful?'

Hope of the Unseen

Does the church still want to insist in walking by sight? 2 Corinthians 5:7 says "For we walk by faith and not by sight". What does faith offer that sight does not? It's also interesting to note
that the statement 'the just live by faith' appears four times throughout the bible. It's as though God was trying to communicate a standard; this being - if you're just, then you are to live by faith.

Question is, what is faith? Hebrews 11:1 reveals a mystery of this question. "Now faith is the substance of things hoped for, the evidence of things not seen". The mystery I want us to focus on here is 'not seen or unseen'. You can also say 'the evidence of things invisible'. Dictionary defines invisible as "that which cannot be seen". Which is true to most in this world but doesn't have to be true to us. There are another set of eyes belonging to the heart. Eyes that have the capacity to behold the invisible realm. Faith is really laying hold of what is unseen and dragging it into the seen by whatever means necessary. Our hope comes from what we do not yet see. Romans 8:24-25 reads "For we were saved in this hope, but hope that is seen is not hope; for why does one still hope for what he see. But if we hope for what we do not see, we eagerly wait for it with perseverance".

The Eagle's Anointing

At this point I look at my watch, and I peer over God's calendar. By divine calculation, we understand that it's just about time for universal change to take place. The Bride is about to have a 'glorified' makeover and have every wrinkle ironed out. The church has cried out for a Deliverer, and behold it will be The Lord Himself, coming in the power of His Spirit. Ephesians 5:26 says He's coming back for a glorious bride, without spot and wrinkle and we also know that EVERY prophecy given by His Word will be fulfilled.

At this point I mention the God Assignment. Name: Operation Eagle's Anointing. Mission: To empower the children of God to take off the ground and fly into the realm of God. To transition from the third dimension to the fourth dimension, from the earth into heaven. This anointing is an end-time gift from God to the church which prevents us from living by our eye-sight. It's a gift that opens up our heart- sight. This gift came with the wings of eagles to soar to heavenly heights and to travel with rocket speed, too fast and too high for enemy birds. This gift gives razor sharp vision and ability to survey the land with great detail, from a great distance. It enables us to see into the eternal realm of God's Kingdom and makes us to have a 'God's-eye view' to the world beneath.

The Dynamics of the Eagle

The eagle is truly a dynamic bird. It's a bird than can see up to 5 miles in detail. It can zero in on its moving target prey from 2 miles above the ground. It blocks out the surrounding environment and auto-locks its focus onto its potential meal. It can see fish under water from hundreds of feet high. The eagle has remarkable vision. Job 39:28-29 informs us that "On the rock it dwells and resides, on the crag of the rock and the stronghold, from there it spies out the prey; its eyes observe from afar.

"The eagle has an extraordinary perception much greater than a man of perfect vision. It can travel at ferocious speed that even the bible when trying to convey the idea of great speed, says in Deut 28:49 "The Lord will bring a nation against you from afar, from the end of the earth, as swift as the eagle flies". Also in 2 Samuel 1:23 "Saul and Jonathan were beloved and pleasant in their lives, and they were not divided. They were swifter than eagles and stronger than lions".

By knowing the characteristics of the eagle, we can begin to comprehend the awesome abilities that the eagle's anointing will give us, the heirs of salvation. Looking at vision, no longer will we be bound to the seen, but we will operate in the realm of the unseen, becoming aware of what is happening behind the scenes, and gazing upon the future plans of God. When we use the word vision we could also use the word perception. This is key because perception doesn't just mean what we can see, but also what is revealed and what we can understand. Those who have acute perception will receive acute revelation. These will have what Jesus would say 'eyes to see'. Jesus wasn't just relating to seeing invisible things but also eyes that comprehend and grasp the mysteries of God's word and Kingdom. Also in the Greek text of the scripture, when the word for understand is used, the description given is "To piece together". Those with the eagle's oil will have the ability piece together puzzle pieces of knowledge that they may comprehend the bigger picture. The higher you fly the greater the area your eyes can cover and see.

Unveiling Mysteries
Ephesians 1: "I pray that the God of our Lord Jesus Christ, the Father of glory, may give to you the spirit of wisdom and revelation in the knowledge of Him, the eyes of your understanding being enlightened..." Paul said "eyes of your understanding being enlightened". Some translations say "eyes of your heart". Light in the bible is mainly symbolic for knowledge. Knowledge meaning awareness being opposite to darkness which often is symbolic for ignorance.

To paraphrase in Paul's prayer he was saying ***"I pray that knowledge will flood your heart by the spirit of wisdom and revelation, that your eyes can perceive truth so you're no longer ignorant God's plans and purposes".***

Taking all this into consideration, we realize that those of the eagles anointing will be swept up by the wind of the spirit of wisdom and revelation, which is a manifestation of the Holy Spirit. In these last days those of the eagle nature will have the ability to search out mysteries that God conceals not from His children, but for His children, mysteries not revealed to man (Proverbs 25:2). When revelation was given to Daniel, the angel instructed him to go his way because the mysteries given were sealed
until the time of the end (Daniel 12:9). Well, we are in the time of the end and the Lord has broken and still is breaking the seals of the scrolls that His sons may behold profound secrets. Secrets that carry so much weight of glory.

Habakkuk 2:14 declares: ***"For the earth will be filled with the knowledge of the glory of the Lord, as the waters cover the sea".***

It's vitally important we understand this scripture that we might enter into the 'Glory Realm'.

Remembering that knowledge means awareness, makes us to realize that the glory is around us, but we have yet to become aware of it. To put it quite simply I would say: No knowledge, no Glory! The glory is hidden and invisible and it takes those who know how to search for and seek God to reveal it on earth. It's for those who can see and believe the invisible becoming visible. Those who have sharp perception to attain the knowledge of the glory will then be able to plug into it, causing earth to align with heaven. **Now, let the redeem of the Lord say so: Amen!**

Those Who Wait on The Lord

It's a well-known fact that for eagle's to saw to extreme heights they wait for a strong rushing wind that propels them. They don't just take off when they feel any wind either, but they wait upon a forceful wind by discerning the strength of it.

Isaiah 40:31 reads: *"But those who wait on the Lord Shall renew their strength; They shall mount up with wings like eagles, they shall run and not be weary, they shall walk and not faint"*. In other words those who wait upon the wind of the Lord shall be empowered to mount up on high, have enduring speed and strength without becoming weary.

The eagles of God will have the God given ability to ascend to various peaks of the mountains of society and challenge those who control the systems of this world. They will be instructed with <u>a mandate to challenge</u> those who oppose God's Kingdom and cause a rearrangement to take place in the spirit then natural. They will be equipped with great insight and delegated with authority from Christ who has authority of all things, to conquer the various powers that be who seduce the nations and lead them astray, preventing the gospel of the Kingdom being known. It will only be eagles that can reach these mountain peaks of society.

Daniel and Joseph carried such an anointing as they were elevated by God to great influential positions in heathen nations. Both carried deep prophetic insight and had a wealth of understanding much greater than mere men.

This anointing is the engine of the prophetic. It keeps us active, energetic, constantly changing and in motion. Revelation 8:13 says: And I looked, and I heard an angel flying through the midst of heaven, saying with a loud voice, "Woe, woe, woe to the inhabitants of the earth, because of the remaining blasts of the trumpet of the three angels who are about to sound!" Here we see that those of the eagle kind shall not be subject to the woes of the earth as well as knowing the prophetic calendar of God.

Those of the eagle's anointing don't live on the ground of the earth; they soar through the heavenlies and nest on God's Holy Mountain. Heaven is truly the home for them because they have the ability to fly there at will.

In conclusion I realize that the earth has plenty of carnality and sensuality, the church do not need to contribute to the abundance of it.

Jesus has elected His remnant and they'll be equipped with every gift and blessing needed to fulfill His Plans and Purposes. Nothing by no means will prevent His sovereignty; He will be glorified, AMEN. The Lord will have His servants trained in the eagle's anointing to accomplish that which He has ordained them to do.

He will send them into the systems of this world with great wisdom and understanding, enduring speed and strength, partnered with authority from the government of Heaven. Their mind will be set on things above, so to be earthly/carnally minded, will be too low for the eagle to rest or fly.

It's true that these are the people of God that live in heaven and visit earth.

Amen. Even so, come, Lord Jesus.

The Grace of our Lord Jesus Christ be with you all. Amen!

Prophet Christ Mondzali

www.ingramcontent.com/pod-product-compliance
Lightning Source LLC
Chambersburg PA
CBHW080744300426
44114CB00019B/2644